# "Congress shall make no law ... abridging the freedom of speech, or of the press."

*First Amendment to the US Constitution*

The basic foundation of our democracy is the First Amendment guarantee of freedom of expression. The Opposing Viewpoints series is dedicated to the concept of this basic freedom and the idea that it is more important to practice it than to enshrine it.

# OPPOSING VIEWPOINTS® SERIES

# Green Politics

## M. M. Eboch, Book Editor

GREENHAVEN PUBLISHING

Published in 2022 by Greenhaven Publishing, LLC
353 3rd Avenue, Suite 255, New York, NY 10010

**Library of Congress Cataloging-in-Publication Data**

Names: Eboch, M. M., editor.
Title: Green politics / M. M. Eboch, Book Editor.
Description: First edition. | New York : Greenhaven Publishing, [2022] |
  Series: Opposing viewpoints | Includes bibliographical references and
  index. | Contents: Green politics | Audience: Ages 15+ | Audience:
  Grades 10–12 | Summary: "Anthology of essays exploring Green Politics
  and environmental policy"— Provided by publisher.
Identifiers: LCCN 2021037214 | ISBN 9781534508439 (library binding) | ISBN
  9781534508422 (paperback)
Subjects: LCSH: Environmentalism—Juvenile literature. | Environmental
  policy—Juvenile literature. | Green Movement—Juvenile literature.
Classification: LCC GE195.5 .G74 2022 | DDC 320.58—dc23
LC record available at https://lccn.loc.gov/2021037214

*Manufactured in the United States of America*

Website: http://greenhavenpublishing.com

# Contents

# The Importance of Opposing Viewpoints

Perhaps every generation experiences a period in time in which the populace seems especially polarized, starkly divided on the important issues of the day and gravitating toward the far ends of the political spectrum and away from a consensus-facilitating middle ground. The world that today's students are growing up in and that they will soon enter into as active and engaged citizens is deeply fragmented in just this way. Issues relating to terrorism, immigration, women's rights, minority rights, race relations, health care, taxation, wealth and poverty, the environment, policing, military intervention, the proper role of government—in some ways, perennial issues that are freshly and uniquely urgent and vital with each new generation—are currently roiling the world.

If we are to foster a knowledgeable, responsible, active, and engaged citizenry among today's youth, we must provide them with the intellectual, interpretive, and critical-thinking tools and experience necessary to make sense of the world around them and of the all-important debates and arguments that inform it. After all, the outcome of these debates will in large measure determine the future course, prospects, and outcomes of the world and its peoples, particularly its youth. If they are to become successful members of society and productive and informed citizens, students need to learn how to evaluate the strengths and weaknesses of someone else's arguments, how to sift fact from opinion and fallacy, and how to test the relative merits and validity of their own opinions against the known facts and the best possible available information. The landmark series Opposing Viewpoints has been providing students with just such critical-thinking skills and exposure to the debates surrounding society's most urgent contemporary issues for many years, and it continues to serve this essential role with undiminished commitment, care, and rigor.

The key to the series's success in achieving its goal of sharpening students' critical-thinking and analytic skills resides in its title—

Opposing Viewpoints. In every intriguing, compelling, and engaging volume of this series, readers are presented with the widest possible spectrum of distinct viewpoints, expert opinions, and informed argumentation and commentary, supplied by some of today's leading academics, thinkers, analysts, politicians, policy makers, economists, activists, change agents, and advocates. Every opinion and argument anthologized here is presented objectively and accorded respect. There is no editorializing in any introductory text or in the arrangement and order of the pieces. No piece is included as a "straw man," an easy ideological target for cheap point-scoring. As wide and inclusive a range of viewpoints as possible is offered, with no privileging of one particular political ideology or cultural perspective over another. It is left to each individual reader to evaluate the relative merits of each argument— as he or she sees it, and with the use of ever-growing critical-thinking skills—and grapple with his or her own assumptions, beliefs, and perspectives to determine how convincing or successful any given argument is and how the reader's own stance on the issue may be modified or altered in response to it.

This process is facilitated and supported by volume, chapter, and selection introductions that provide readers with the essential context they need to begin engaging with the spotlighted issues, with the debates surrounding them, and with their own perhaps shifting or nascent opinions on them. In addition, guided reading and discussion questions encourage readers to determine the authors' point of view and purpose, interrogate and analyze the various arguments and their rhetoric and structure, evaluate the arguments' strengths and weaknesses, test their claims against available facts and evidence, judge the validity of the reasoning, and bring into clearer, sharper focus the reader's own beliefs and conclusions and how they may differ from or align with those in the collection or those of their classmates.

Research has shown that reading comprehension skills improve dramatically when students are provided with compelling, intriguing, and relevant "discussable" texts. The subject matter of these collections could not be more compelling, intriguing, or urgently relevant to today's students and the world they are poised to inherit. The anthologized articles and the reading and discussion questions that are included with them also provide the basis for stimulating, lively, and passionate classroom debates. Students who are compelled to anticipate objections to their own argument and identify the flaws in those of an opponent read more carefully, think more critically, and steep themselves in relevant context, facts, and information more thoroughly. In short, using discussable text of the kind provided by every single volume in the Opposing Viewpoints series encourages close reading, facilitates reading comprehension, fosters research, strengthens critical thinking, and greatly enlivens and energizes classroom discussion and participation. The entire learning process is deepened, extended, and strengthened.

For all of these reasons, Opposing Viewpoints continues to be exactly the right resource at exactly the right time—when we most need to provide readers with the critical-thinking tools and skills that will not only serve them well in school but also in their careers and their daily lives as decision-making family members, community members, and citizens. This series encourages respectful engagement with and analysis of opposing viewpoints and fosters a resulting increase in the strength and rigor of one's own opinions and stances. As such, it helps make readers "future ready," and that readiness will pay rich dividends for the readers themselves, for the citizenry, for our society, and for the world at large.

# Introduction

> *"Greens put the common good before corporate greed, and the public interest before private profit. Forging a red-green synthesis, they integrate policies for social justice with policies for tackling the life-threatening dangers posed by global warming, environmental pollution, resource depletion and species extinction."*
>
> —Peter Tatchell, "Why I Joined the Greens," Green Party

In some ways, America's Green Party may not seem very important. Its membership is only around 250,000. Compare that to some 47 million Democrats and 35 million Republicans in 2020. The Green Party has never gotten a candidate elected to a federal office. Howie Hawkins, the Green Party's presidential candidate in the 2020 election, got only about 0.2 percent of the votes.

Yet the Green Party is more active at the local level, with party members holding office on city councils, on school boards, and occasionally as mayor or representatives at the state level. In addition, the Green Party speaks out strongly on environmental and social justice issues. Young people tend to be more concerned with these issues. That could mean the Green Party has a chance to grow in the future.

The party has been blamed—wrongly, some experts say—for the Democrats losing prior presidential elections. In the 2020 election, some Republican groups tried to get the Green Party on state ballots, hoping to take votes away from the Democrats. Meanwhile, Democrats warned voters not to "waste" a vote on the Green Party, for fear of keeping Donald Trump in office.

In a close political race, one or two percent of the vote could make a difference. In a race for a position as important as US president, many voters don't want to use their vote on a candidate who has no chance of winning. They'd rather vote for a Democrat or Republican, even if their honest first choice would be a third party.

As its name suggests, the Green Party promotes policies for a healthy environment. In the 1970s, various environmentalist political parties formed around the world. In Europe, Greens first organized as an anti-nuclear, pro-peace movement. West Germany founded the first national party, die Grünen, in 1979. By 1990, nearly every country in western and northern Europe had a party with an environmental focus and "Green" in the name. Green parties also arose in Canada, New Zealand, Australia, Argentina, and Chile. The movement eventually spread to eastern Europe as well.

In the United States, the Green Party dates back to 1984. Three women and two men who were involved in politics or environmental action designed a Founding Conference for the Green Party. They invited activist organizations working for issues such as ecology, social justice, civil rights, peace, feminism, and veterans' rights. Sixty-two activists attended the three-day conference. This eventually led to the founding of the Green Party of the United States.

After the conference, participants began drafting a statement on the party's "Ten Key Values." The original Ten Key Values were ecological wisdom, personal and social responsibility, grassroots democracy, nonviolence, decentralization, community-based economics, post-patriarchal values, respect for diversity, global responsibility, and future focus. The wording on some values was later changed. For example, post-patriarchal values became feminism and/or gender equity. To the Green Party, protecting the environment is closely linked to social issues. Members believe the key to protecting the planet is dismantling the patriarchal system and the capitalist focus on high profits.

The party grew at the local and state level across the country. This eventually led to the Green Party running a candidate for president, Ralph Nader, in 1996. The son of Lebanese immigrants, Nader is an author and lawyer known for his work on consumer protection. His running mate was Winona LaDuke, an Anishinaabekwe (Ojibwe) Native American who works on environmental and indigenous women's issues. The two appeared on twenty-two state ballots. Nationwide, eighty-two Green candidates ran for political office and twenty-four won elections.

Even this modest success made America's two major parties nervous. The Democrats and Republicans took a firmer hold of their power by making it more difficult for third parties to get on election ballots. Yet many Americans want more choices and believe America needs more major political parties. To achieve that, the entire system of the Electoral College might need to be dismantled. In the meantime, progressive Democrats are taking up some of the Green Party's key issues, though they face obstacles from the more centrist members of their party.

In chapters titled "How Is the Environment Addressed in US Politics?" "Where Do Green Politics Fit into the Political Spectrum?" "Do Americans Need or Want the Green Party?" and "Can Green Politics Become Relevant in America?," *Opposing Viewpoints: The Green Party* explores the Green Party's political views and its relevance in a changing political landscape. The future of American politics could depend on whether third parties such as the Green Party ever get a fair chance at the ballots, and the future of the planet might depend on how Greens can influence the major parties.

# How Is the Environment Addressed in US Politics?

# Chapter Preface

The Green Party is best known for its strong position on the environment. Green Party proposals would attempt to eliminate the use of fossil fuels and end carbon emissions. They would also disarm US nuclear warheads. They would create new environmental programs and organizations and put the public in control of various industries. To pay for these changes, Greens would raise taxes on the wealthy and increase eco-taxes. An eco-tax is a tax on activities considered to be harmful to the environment.

Green Party policies extend to social justice, including LGBTQ protections and antiracism policies. The party proposes to end the war on drugs and mass incarceration, which disproportionately affect people of color. They would also drastically reduce the military. The links between social justice and the environment may not seem immediately obvious. However, advocates of this kind of "eco-socialism" or "green socialism" see a connection. They consider systems such as the patriarchy, racism, and homophobia destructive to people and also to the planet.

While some Green Party members want moderate changes to the current systems, others want to go further. They would ban all fossil fuels in order to eliminate carbon emissions that harm the planet. This would require major changes to US factories and transportation—the vast majority of vehicles currently use fossil fuels.

A Green Party viewpoint that seems extreme to many Americans is the attack on capitalism and consumerism. America has long supported capitalism, where businesses are controlled by owners for profit. This leads to consumerism, the idea that getting people to buy more goods and services is better for those people and the economy as a whole. Modern US consumerism encourages people to buy products they do not need. However, few Americans want to give up their appliances, electronics, toys, and closets full of clothing and shoes.

In less-developed countries, many people aspire to consume more, not less. They are concerned with getting access to safe housing, electricity, clean water, and public transportation. There is a vast gulf between those who have a lot and those who have very little.

Some Green politicians claim that a planned economy is the answer. In a planned economy, the government owns companies and determines prices. This differs from America's current market economy, where most companies are privately owned. Businesses determine prices based on what they can get consumers to pay. The Green Party thinks it can find a balance between saving the environment and giving all people comfortable, enjoyable lives. However, these policies have yet to be widely tested. Critics note that in countries where the Green Party has gained some power, it often ends up compromising with other political parties. Environmental promises are not met and the Green Party does not look very different from other mainstream political parties.

Many Americans support some or all of the Green Party's policies, yet the Green Party has not become a major force in US politics. In part, this is simply because it is extremely hard for any third party to gain power in America. Still, young people now learn about the environment at an early age. Many see global climate change as one of the biggest dangers affecting their future. Young people are also most likely to challenge the system of patriarchy that supports sexism, racism, and homophobia. With more young voters, the Green Party might see greater support for its policies.

The viewpoints in the following chapter look at the Green Party's policies and priorities, especially when it comes to the environment.

*"One of their biggest policies is their promotion of an Ecosocialist Green New Deal...The introduction of these policies would be paid for through the expansion and ramping up of taxes—mostly on the wealthy, but also ecological-based taxes."*

# Ecosocialism Can Improve the World

*Connor Holt*

*In the following viewpoint, Connor Holt describes the political journey and goals of Howie Hawkins. In 2020, Hawkins ran for US president as the Green Party candidate. Angela Walker ran as his vice-presidential candidate. Hawkins and Walker saw ecosocialism as the answer to many of the United States' problems. Ecosocialism, also called green socialism or socialist ecology, imagines a society that is in harmony with nature. To achieve this harmony, ecosocialism works to dismantle destructive systems, such as patriarchy, racism, homophobia, and the globalization of the economy. Connor Holt was a staff writer for the* Daily Beacon, *the campus newspaper of the University of Tennessee Knoxville.*

"Hawkins 2020: The Green Candidate's Beliefs, Campaign Explained," by Connor Holt and the *Daily Beacon*, October 14, 2020. Reprinted by permission.

As you read, consider the following questions:

1. According to this viewpoint, what do Hawkins and Walker want to do to the US military budget?
2. How would their Green Party proposals give communities power over the police?
3. How do racial issues fit into the Green Party's proposals?

H owie Hawkins began his campaign for the office of President of the United States back in 2019. Hawkins began with the goals of building the Green Party's numbers so that it might be seen as a viable opposition to the two current primary parties and to put their stance on issues into the public zeitgeist.

Born in California in 1952, Hawkins was raised in a multicultural neighborhood of San Mateo.

Later, he attended Dartmouth College in Vermont, campaigned for Bernie Sanders's runs for senate and governor of Vermont and joined the Socialist Party in 1973. In the early 90s, he co-founded the Green Party and has run for elected office 24 times unsuccessfully.

Together with vice-presidential pick Angela Walker, the duo seek to bring America to an era of ecosocialism that will fix the failings of the two capitalist parties.

However, the campaign's run for the presidency has seen roadblocks. In September, Hawkins and Walker moved to sue Wisconsin for denying them access to the presidential ballot.

"The Democratic Party is behaving like the anti-Democratic Party by working to keep the Green Party off the ballot. Thousands of voters in Wisconsin reject both former Vice President Joe Biden or President Donald Trump," Walker said. "These voters deserve more choices."

In fact, they've had issues with getting on to the ballot across the country. In New York, for example, the number of votes they needed to remain on the ballot was tripled.

# HOWIE HAWKINS: IN HIS OWN WORDS

In an exclusive conversation with the *Times of India,* the Green Party presidential nominee Howie Hawkins tells us why Democrats are the spoilers, his concerns about the present election process and his take on why Bernie Sanders is now supporting Joe Biden.

**Why do you think Americans should vote for you?**

I say vote for what you support. A lot of people in the Democrat primary supported Bernie Sanders because they want Medicare for all, they want a full-strength green new deal. They want student and medical debt relief. Joe Biden is not for those things. So if they're for those things, they should vote for us. If they vote for Joe Biden, they get lost in the sauce. Nobody knows they are for Medicare for all or a full-strength green new deal (as) they voted for Joe Biden. You vote for the Green Party, your voice is heard and you make the politicians come to you. So that's where your power is—to vote for what you want.

**Why do you think there is a need for a party like yours, the Green Party? Why can't these issues be resolved by the Democrats or the Republicans?**

Well, they're bought and paid for by the wealthy interests, the big corporations. So the economic policies we get benefit the wealthy class, not the working class. So that's why you know public opinion doesn't translate into public policy in this country and that's the fundamental problem of American politics.

**If the two biggest parties of the country, as you say, are bought by the wealthy establishment, how is your party protected from it?**

We do not accept money from for-profit entities, whether it's a business or a trade association. We only take money from regular folks. So lots of little people giving a little bit is how we're gonna compete with the big money.

"US Elections 2020: Democrats Are the Real Spoilers, Not Us, Says Green Party Nominee Howie Hawkins," by Piyush Pal, *Times of India*, July 15, 2020.

Despite this, the campaign and the party has fought for their own right to be considered and for the people's' right to be able to vote for them.

One of their biggest policies is their promotion of an Ecosocialist Green New Deal. Their Green New Deal would include the elimination of all carbon emissions by 2030, a ban on fracking and use of fossil fuels, disarming of all US nuclear warheads, public ownership and planning of various industries and the creation of other environmental programs and organizations.

The introduction of these policies would be paid for through the expansion and ramping up of taxes—mostly on the wealthy, but also ecological-based taxes.

Hawkins would furthermore pull all US troops out of foreign countries.

"We want to cut the military budget by 75% in order to increase our security. The biggest security threat we face is climate change," Hawkins said. "A $250 billion military budget will still be the world's largest. It is far less costly in terms of personnel and weapons to defend a home territory than to invade and occupy foreign territory."

Like Libertarian candidate Jo Jorgenson, Hawkins seeks to end the war on drugs and mass incarceration. He views drug abuse as a health problem rather than a criminal one and would instead mimic the Portuguese model of harm reduction.

This policy falls under the campaign's "Social Justice and Civil Rights" umbrella, which also encompasses various progressive movements for LGBTQ protections, regulations on firearms and the protection of the American people from mass government surveillance.

"We will fight against the prosecution of whistleblowers and publishers under the 1917 Espionage Act, which has always been used for political repression and never more so than during the last two administrations," Hawkins said.

Another way in which Hawkins and Walker seek to preserve the civil rights of Americans is in their policy of community control over the police.

By that, they mean the implementation of community boards that would have real power over the police and would be able to prevent policies such as racial profiling and frisking.

"People are rising up against systemic police violence, especially against Black people. The government should listen to the legitimate concerns of the people. Racism and violence have no place in policing," Walker said.

Along the lines of civil rights, Hawkins supports a single-payer health care system aimed at eliminated the current model of generating profit for a few. His campaign website outlines a multi-phase, decade-long plan for conversion to such a system and the milestone goals each step would achieve.

Hawkins and his party want to usher in an era of peace and prosperity for both America and the world.

Through socialist economic reform, the protection of civil rights and liberties and the stalwart defense of the planet's environment, Hawkins wants to right the wrongs of past administrations and bring justice to the country.

> *"The tendency to put the onus on individuals to change their behavior, rather than fighting for systemic change, means that Greens often support 'green taxes' designed to encourage individuals to modify their behavior."*

# When Greens Compromise, the Planet Suffers

*Hannah Sell*

*In the following viewpoint, Hannah Sell addresses the growing importance of the environment in politics today. Protests against global climate change and other environmental issues have grown around the world. The number of activists advocating for the future of the planet has swelled. Many environmentalists have looked—and continue to look—to the Green Party to defend the planet. However, the author argues, the Green Party has utterly failed to succeed in making improvements to governmental policies on the environment. Instead, the Green Party makes too many compromises, in her view. The author contends that it is impossible to save the planet without addressing the system of capitalism. Hannah Sell is general secretary of the Socialist Party.*

"Green Parties Are Not Enough," by Hannah Sell, Socialist Party, December–January 2015/2016. Reprinted by permission.

As you read, consider the following questions:

1. Why are Green voters often disappointed after their party gains power, according to the author?
2. What happens when people accept the "least bad system," according to this viewpoint?
3. How are economic growth and capitalism connected?

L ast year a massive 400,000 people took part in the US's biggest ever demonstration against global warming. The current ban on demonstrations in France, following the Paris terror attacks, means there are not likely to be such large demonstrations outside December's summit. Globally, however, protests are becoming more common that demand action on climate change as a whole, or oppose specific assaults on their local environment. These include the hundreds of thousands who demonstrated in Stuttgart, Germany, against the Stuttgart 21 rail project. Other recent struggles are the movements against gold mines in Greece, the anti-fracking protests in a whole number of countries including Britain, or the demonstrations against nuclear power in Japan and other countries following the Fukushima disaster of 2011.

For many of those who become active in environmental movements it is natural to look for a political expression for their protests. Those participating in the Greek protests against the gold mines initially turned in the main to Syriza. One of the many results of the Syriza leadership's capitulation to the demands of the troika and global capitalism was a betrayal of these environmental protesters.

In many cases, however, environmental protestors look to the Greens to give their views an electoral expression. Many Green parties initially arose out of struggles in defence of the planet. The German Greens (Die Grünen), for a long time the strongest Green Party, emerged from the mass movements against nuclear power in the 1970s and 1980s. The same is true of Sweden's Green Party (Miljöpartiet de gröna).

In some countries it is not only those motivated primarily by environmental issues who are attracted to the Greens. In England and Wales their membership quadrupled in 2015 and they received over a million votes in the general election, primarily because they were seen as more left wing and anti-austerity than the three major parties. The election of anti-austerity Jeremy Corbyn as leader of the Labour Party has now cut across this trend but, depending on the outcome of the struggle between pro- and anti-austerity forces in the Labour Party, the Greens could again become a major beneficiary of the anti-austerity mood in society.

## Ecological Compromise

While Green parties may often be perceived as both the best fighters in defense of the environment and as on the left on social issues, their record in government tells a different tale. In Stuttgart, for example, the Greens had a significant electoral surge as a result of the movement and formed a coalition with the former social democrats, the SPD, in 2009. However, the SPD was pro-Stuttgart 21 and so the net result of Green participation in the coalition was only to win agreement on holding a referendum on whether it should go ahead. Following a huge campaign from big business, the Greens lost the referendum.

Stuttgart is just one local example of a general trend. From the early 1990s up to 2015, European Green parties have participated in national government in 21 countries: Belgium, Bulgaria, Czech Republic, Denmark, Estonia, Finland, France, Georgia, Germany, Greece, Ireland, Italy, Latvia, Lithuania, Luxembourg, Poland, Romania, Slovakia, Slovenia, Sweden and Ukraine. Many of these were "red-green" coalitions with ex-social democratic parties, but by no means all. In the Czech Republic, Latvia and Ireland, Greens entered coalitions with right-wing capitalist parties. The Greens have also taken part in government outside of Europe, including in Brazil, Mauritius and Kenya.

On not a single occasion has such participation led to qualitative improvements in government policy on the environment. The

German Greens, for example, were in government coalition with the SPD for seven years from 1998 to 2005. In that time the number of wind farms increased significantly but by 2005, according to the World Wildlife Fund, nine of the 30 most harmful European coal plants were found in Germany, five in the top ten. One was in second place, just behind Greece. Having come to prominence in the anti-nuclear power movement, the German Greens in government signed up to a deal for nuclear power to be eliminated over the following 20 to 30 years, effectively guaranteeing the nuclear power industry a secure future for decades.

In France, the Greens (Europe Écologie—Les Verts) took part in a coalition with the Parti Socialiste, along with others, from 1997 to 2002. Securing the environment ministry, the Greens effectively abandoned their opposition to nuclear power. In Ireland, the Greens joined a coalition with Fianna Fáil and promptly acquiesced to Shell Oil getting permission to develop the Corrib gas field off Ireland's west coast. There had been a mass campaign against this, previously vocally supported by the Greens. While Shell got permission to drill, environmental protesters who had campaigned against them were left languishing in prison.

## A Woeful Role

It is not only on environmental issues that Greens have played a woeful role in government. The Irish Greens accepted other measures that they had campaigned against in opposition, including the use of Shannon airport by the US military for "renditions"—the forced removal of suspects to secret locations for interrogation. Having opposed incinerators, they then oversaw the building of one of the biggest in western Europe.

All of the governments the Greens have participated in have been in the age of neoliberalism and have—to a greater or lesser extent—overseen privatization, deregulation and attacks on workers' rights. The red-green coalition in Germany presided over the introduction of the Hartz IV laws and €1 jobs—the biggest attack on welfare and workers' living standards since the Second World War.

In Ireland, the Greens in government initially signed up to the EU/IMF savage austerity, including the household charge, water charges, VAT hikes and major public spending cuts, only belatedly pulling out as their poll results reached vanishing point. In France, over five years, the "plural left" government privatized more than previous conservative governments. Air France and Air Inter were privatized, and the national rail company, SNCF, was partly dismantled.

In Italy, the Greens (Verdi) signed up in 2007 to the then prime minister's program for "liberalization" (ie privatization) of public services, and immediate action to cut the public sector. Since the Romano Prodi-led coalition collapsed, the Greens have disappeared as an electoral force in Italian politics. Per Gahrton, the author of *Green Parties, Green Future: From Local Groups to the International Stage*, comments: "It is impossible to know if the electoral losses and the eradication of the Greens as an independent force in Italian politics is related to their participation in government, or rather an effect of the chaotic political landscape in the country." In fact, it is an iron law that Greens suffer electoral losses as a result of government participations, as their largely left-wing electorate is disillusioned by the grubby reality of Green representatives seeming to sell their souls for a ministerial portfolio or two.

## Mind the Gap

Why is the gap so big between the radical aspirations of many Green voters and members, and the reality of the Greens in government? At root it is related to their attitude to capitalism. Green parties' central motivation is saving the planet. However, generally, their leaderships do not conclude that ending environmental degradation is linked to ending capitalism. Some do not even define themselves as being on the left. The Brazilian Greens (Partido Verde) clearly say: "PV does not accept the narrow polarization between left and right, we are in front." What does "in front" mean?

As Per Gahrton expresses it: "Most Green parties explicitly accept private ownership and the market economy—less as a matter of principle, more because such an economy is considered the least bad system known." The net result of accepting what they believe is "the least bad" system has been a preparedness to join capitalist governments in the hope of getting a few concessions for the environment, while ending up agreeing to policies that are in the interests of capitalism but are a disaster for the environment, humanity and the Green Party!

Many Green parties support some limited nationalization. In the 2015 general election in Britain, for example, the Greens stood for re-nationalization of the railways—although not the energy companies, banks, or wider industry. Globally, however, their record when in power has been to abandon these pledges and to acquiesce to further privatization of public services.

Rather than capitalism itself, Green parties lay the blame for climate change with consumerism and economic growth. The Italian Greens put it in their program as follows: "A Green is someone who sees in economic growth the original cause of the degradation of our planet." However, they are not able to explain how they intend to end economic growth without ending capitalism, which has the drive for unplanned and wasteful growth written into its DNA.

Unsurprisingly, opposition to economic growth is held less firmly by Green parties in the neo-colonial world. The Benin Greens say, for example: "To be able to travel in all Africa, locally as well as internationally, the Beninians should be able to dream about bicycles, normal trains, express trains or airplanes, under comfortable and secure conditions."

## The Need for Economic Planning

This sums up one of the difficulties of the Greens' condemnation of economic growth. For much of the world's population, economic growth is vitally needed. Worldwide, 1.3 billion people still do not have access to electricity. More than 700 million have no access to clean water. On a world scale, capitalism is not providing even the basic elements of civilization to billions. Workers not only in Benin but throughout large parts of Africa and Asia dream of a modern transport system, along with decent housing, electrification and so on.

Equally, condemnation of "consumerism" in the economically developed capitalist countries is one-sided. Of course it is true that modern capitalism encourages people to buy ever more unnecessary products. Nonetheless, many consumer goods genuinely improve the lives of working-class people. Fridges, vacuum cleaners and washing machines, all improve people's lives, particularly those of women who continue to shoulder most of the burden of domestic work. They are part of the accumulated standard of living of sections of the working class, won through the struggles of previous decades.

But is it possible to support economic growth in order to meet the needs of humanity, while at the same time preventing the destruction of the planet? Not on the basis of capitalism. Capitalism's relentless drive for profit and its inbuilt need for economic growth have already wreaked havoc on our environment, bringing the world close to catastrophe. The current Tory government in Britain is systematically getting rid of the few measures to encourage renewable power that previously existed. This is no surprise given the character of British capitalism—a third of the current value of the London Stock Exchange is made up of "high-carbon" energy and mining companies.

However, a democratic socialist planned economy—based on bringing the major corporations into democratic public ownership—would be able to plan economic growth in order to meet the needs of humanity and also to protect the planet. With massive investment into renewable energy, the link between economic growth and environmental degradation could be broken. Moreover, a socialist planned economy, organised to meet humanity's needs rather than an insatiable thirst for private profit, would not have an "inbuilt" need for continual economic expansion.

The tendency to put the onus on individuals to change their behavior, rather than fighting for systemic change, means that Greens often support "green taxes" designed to encourage individuals to modify their behavior. However, these are often regressive, hitting the poorest sections of society hardest. Motorway toll charges, congestion charges and fuel taxes are not the most effective means to stop people using their cars, for example, when many people have no other means of getting from A to B. Fighting for a high-quality free or very cheap public transport system would have a far greater effect. This, however, means coming up against the interests of big business.

## Non-Class Approach

The Greens globally do not see society in class terms. Per Gahrton writes: "Class or national solidarity is basically a kind of egocentrism, demanding that people feel solidarity with other people of their own type, social or national." In Britain, the Greens have criticized the historic links between the Labour Party and the trade unions, and have supported the right wing of the party's destruction of these links. Caroline Lucas, the Green MP, praised the Collins Review, which removed the last vestiges of the collective voice of the unions within the Labour Party. She wrote: "To his credit, Ed Miliband has inched towards some kind of reform. So too have some union leaders, who perhaps see they would have more influence if they were not so clearly tied to one party—just like the RSPB [Royal Society for the Protection of Birds] can campaign effectively for birds, whoever is in power" (*Honourable Friends: Parliament and the Fight for Change*).

No doubt Caroline Lucas would like more trade unionists to join the Greens, but there is no room in the Green Party constitution for organisations, including trade unions, to affiliate to it or have any kind of collective voice. Ultimately, by opposing the existence of a party that represents the collective interests of the working class, the Greens are arguing that the choice should be between different parties representing the interests of the capitalist class.

Socialists' support for "class solidarity" is not egocentrism, but science. It is a recognition that the working class is responsible for the creation of the capitalists' profits and that by collective action it is capable of bringing capitalist society to a halt but also, potentially, of building a new socialist, non-environment-degrading society. The struggle for such a society can win solidarity from many beyond the ranks of the working class, even from individuals from very privileged backgrounds who recognize that only by fighting for socialism will it be possible to save the planet.

## Abstract Internationalism

Recognizing that the environmental crisis is a global crisis the Greens correctly emphasize the need for global solutions. This approach is their justification for promoting "international institutions" such as the European Union (EU) and the Eurozone. Following the nightmare imposed on the Greek people by the institutions of the EU, most Greens emphasized the need to "reform" the EU, but they have no concrete proposals on how it is possible to reform the completely undemocratic big-business club that is the EU. The Volkswagen emissions tests scandal shows in sharp relief how the EU does not act to protect the environment, or the lungs of its inhabitants, but the corporate interests of major European companies.

Yet the Greens have a long history of not only supporting the EU but of signing up to many of its neoliberal charters. The Greens in the European parliament, for example, called for support for the 2007 Lisbon treaty, which included a whole raft of privatization, deregulation and attacks on workers' rights. They explained their position by saying: "The Greens in the European parliament support the treaty of Lisbon as a further step in the European constitutional process…It is a compromise, and in many ways an unsatisfactory one, however it is indispensable and represents a step forward."

Probably, many Greens thought it was a necessary, "internationalist" measure to support the Lisbon treaty. But, of course, by backing attempts of big business to impose unity from above in their own interests—replete with privatization and attacks on workers' rights—the Greens have only helped to fuel the inevitable anger against the EU that has developed in countries across Europe.

## Socialist Greens

Per Gahrton may consider "national solidarity" to be a kind of egocentrism, but that is not how Greek, Portuguese or Irish workers would see it, facing the driving down of their living conditions in the name of the EU, which acts almost as a colonial power. A genuine internationalist approach means being prepared to break with capitalism and to fight for a democratic, socialist Europe.

While the leadership of the Green parties worldwide have consistently ended up supporting neoliberal measures when in power, that does not mean that all their members agree. In many countries, anti-capitalists and socialists have joined Green parties. In England and Wales, where the electoral system means that the Greens have not yet been tested on a national basis, Greens have nonetheless shared power at local level with parties of all political stripes. In Brighton council, the Greens formed a minority administration for four years from 2011. Unfortunately, that council consistently implemented the austerity policies demanded by the national Tory-led government, resulting in their losing power in 2015. However, a minority of the Green councillors did take a principled stand and refused to vote for further cuts in public services.

This is a small indication of how forces inside Green parties can play a role in forming part of the kind of "real Green" parties that are needed. Such parties would have to stand unequivocally against the capitalist system that is destroying the planet, and be parties of the working class and oppressed worldwide. They would need to fight for democratic socialism as the only means to both permanently end austerity and halt the degradation of our environment.

> *"The Green Party remains to a large extent a fringe movement, not a political force to be reckoned with."*

# The Green Party Should Get Back to the Environment

*Remco Van Der Stoep*

*In the following excerpted viewpoint, Remco Van Der Stoep explores the Green Party's activity in the United Kingdom. One Green Party candidate was elected to the national legislature as an MP (member of Parliament) in 2010. However, that victory failed to lead to further political success. The author explores why that happened and how the Green Party might change its focus for more success. She takes ideas from Emiliano Grossman, an associate professor of politics, and explores how they might be adapted to Great Britain. The UK Labour Party is closer to the US Democrats, while Boris Johnson's conservative "Brexit Party" aligns more closely with US Republicans. Brexit was the withdrawal of the United Kingdom from the European Union in 2020. Author Remco Van Der Stoep has been involved in the Green Party of England and Wales for more than a decade.*

"From Stagnation to Transformation: Where Next for the Green Party," by Remco Van Der Stoep, Open Democracy, January 22, 2020. Reprinted by permission.

As you read, consider the following questions:

1. How did the UK Green Party try to collaborate with other political parties in 2017?
2. Why and how should the Green Party refocus on the environment, according to this viewpoint?
3. What is the difference between winning arguments versus winning seats in government?

Would Caroline Lucas, or indeed anyone in the Green Party, have guessed back in 2010, when Lucas won the Brighton Pavilion seat and became the UK's first Green MP, that three general elections on, she would still be the party's sole representative in the House of Commons?

It was widely believed that once the party had made its initial breakthrough under first-past-the-post, the road to a steadily growing Westminster representation would be open. Now, three fruitless attempts on, it's time for a rethink.

The situation is one of great irony. The Greens' policies and priorities have been consistent over the past decade—much more so than those of other progressive parties—and they are being vindicated in many ways, not least by seeing much of their 2015 manifesto transposed into subsequent Labour Party manifestos, with the notable exception of the Greens' commitment to electoral reform.

Environmental concerns are becoming a priority for the electorate, reflected in a campaign that saw Channel 4 host a dedicated climate debate and other parties attempting to out-green the Greens. The website Vote for Policies consistently finds that the Green Party's policies are among the most popular, with one in five people seeking voting advice there receiving a recommendation to vote Green. The Green Party's aims and work are getting increasing recognition from civil society organisations and public figures. Clearly, it is doing something right. But being a political party, the only real currency is that of votes, and however much vindication and sympathy it receives, it won't feel like accomplishment until it translates into more Green MPs.

Of course, Westminster elections aren't the only measure of electoral success and the Green Party has seen some decent results over recent years. The party doubled its number of councillors in the past year and now has more local representation than ever before, and the 2019 European election saw the Greens take 12 percent of the vote nationally, giving the party seven MEPs. There's also the success of the Scottish Greens, a separate party, whose six MSPs currently hold the balance of power in Holyrood, holding a minority SNP government to account, and two Green Assembly members now lead the opposition against the cross-community government in Northern Ireland's newly reconvened Assembly. But in the public eye—partly due to chronic underrepresentation in mainstream media coverage—the Green Party remains to a large extent a fringe movement, not a political force to be reckoned with. It's hard to see how that will change if not through general election success.

## Learning and Adapting in a Tight Space

To some commentators, the absence of further general election success stories—aside from the ever-growing majority Caroline Lucas enjoys in her Brighton Pavilion constituency—is down to a failure of strategy, leadership, or both, at the heart of the Green Party. Such criticisms are overly harsh, as well as lazy. They fail to recognise that within the limited breathing space available to the party, it has done reasonably well to learn and adapt, general election after general election.

Between 2010 and 2015 the party built its local presence across England and Wales and carved out a space to the left of the Labour Party, which, helped by a favourable public mood, culminated in the "Green surge"—a mass flock of new members to the party and, eventually, its best ever general election result in terms of national vote share—3.8 percent.

What the Green surge didn't produce was additional Green Party MPs. Incidentally, it also boosted the number of progressive tragedy constituencies—seats where a Tory MP got elected only because the split of the progressive vote. So, in 2017, as Labour under Corbyn had moved considerably in the Green direction, and the Tories had become populist hard-Brexit advocates, the Green Party embraced the Progressive Alliance—to stop a Tory landslide and, just as much, to demonstrate the power and potential of collaboration in politics. It was hoped that by doing the right thing, hearts and minds within Labour and beyond would be won over, with electoral reform as the prize.

Despite the considerable impact of the Progressive Alliance, it was not to be. The Green Party's own vote share collapsed, and Labour's tribal instincts told it to aim for the remaining Green votes, rather than acknowledging the virtue and the potential of progressive cross-party collaboration. A bruising experience for the party and many of its supporters, but one that allowed it to find new strength, as the seed of the Progressive Alliance was not going to un-sow itself. It was, in fact, germinating in various places and in various ways.

Come 2019 the Greens found themselves bolstered by a "European Green Wave," and its bold stance on Brexit and climate breakdown contributed to unprecedented electoral success in local and European elections that year—possibly boosted in part by voters who opted to reward the Green Party for its constructive attitude to the Progressive Alliance in 2017. And indeed, local progressive alliances with Liberal Democrats and others had something to do with the many gains made in the local elections. This in turn paved the way for what was eventually known as "Unite to Remain"—a bold electoral pact that the Green Party agreed with the Lib Dems and Plaid Cymru, involving 60 constituencies across England and Wales.

Unite to Remain was in many ways a natural successor to the Progressive Alliance, but crucially for the Green Party, this alliance was more equitable, with the Greens running on behalf of the three-party alliance in ten constituencies. Faced with the familiar barrier of the first-past-the-post (FPTP) voting system and on the back of the strong showing in the European elections, participating in Unite to Remain was clearly the right thing to do for the Green Party, offering the best available route to electoral progress.

The tragedy is that, for its main purpose, it didn't work—none of the participating parties increased their seats tally. But to say that therefore, the pact itself was a failure, is to ignore the complex reality of the campaign and the result. The Green Party's best results were in seats where it was backed by Unite to Remain. While in other seats its vote went up by an average of just one percent, in Unite to Remain-backed seats there was an average vote share increase of 6.9 percent. The Green Party came second in two constituencies; both of these were Unite to Remain seats. Crumbs, perhaps, but a clear indication that the pact enhanced the realm of what was—or would have been—electorally possible.

The depressing bottom line, however, is that the prospect of further Green Party MPs entering the House of Commons under the current electoral system remains remote. There have been Green surges and waves, progressive and Remain alliances—their impact has been felt and lasts to this day—but being a Green MP in Westminster remains a lonely affair for Caroline Lucas. So, what should the party do now?

## Three Strategic Choices

First of all, the Green Party needs to carry out a serious and brutally honest review of its 2019 election strategy and campaign. It should ask itself the difficult questions and ask them until there is a full and satisfactory response to each of them. Why didn't the election give us further Green MPs? Why did the broad public support for climate action not translate in many more Green votes? How did we spend more money on lost deposits than we received in donations? What caused so many of those who voted Green in local and European elections to vote differently in the general election?

On that last question, a recent article by Emiliano Grossman in the *Green European Journal* makes some interesting points. He writes about the French Greens, but the picture is quite similar. Grossman believes that Greens need to make three strategic choices to persuade voters to stick with them in national elections, and the first one is about putting the environment front and centre again.

## Ecological Prism

His concern is that in their pursuit of recognition as a full political party in its own right, Greens have ceded ground to others on the big themes of climate and environment. This is certainly true in the UK context—even if the Greens' policies are still the most ambitious. Now that climate and environmental issues increasingly guide people's voting behaviour, the Green Party must be recognised and trusted as the obvious political force to address voters' concerns. For the party, that means finding the confidence for a bold change of tone; the confidence to be its ecological self. Not by neglecting other themes, but by framing them, as Grossman puts it, "through an ecological prism." To that I would add that this prism should work both ways, and that the power of our green narrative depends on its ability to encompass equality, social and racial justice, and democracy.

## An Outward-Looking Party

The second strategic choice Grossman identifies is about becoming more open and outward-looking, especially vis-à-vis younger generations. The Greens often say that they are, or want to be, the political wing of the climate movement, and their politicians certainly put in the extra mile to support activists from Extinction Rebellion, the youth climate strike movement, and the wider environmentalist movement. Nevertheless, that seemingly small and logical step from supporting climate activism to voting Green—not to mention joining the Green Party—isn't yet commonplace. And while there are many factors at work here, some of it may well be down to the party itself.

Green Party activism could be much more rooted in communities and civil society, and a good deal more accommodating to people with diverse backgrounds and interests than it has been in recent years. In my view, the culprit is the party hierarchy's obsession with a reasonably effective method for winning seats in local elections, dubbed "target to win." Somehow, over time this has evolved from a method to a philosophy, and the first thing a new activist will be briefed about as they come along to their first local party gathering. Enter the Green Party and you enter a tunnel at the end of which there is an extra Green councillor at the next local election.

It's easy to see how—while the prospect may be an attractive one to some—this can be a turn-off for those whose activism is driven by deep concerns about the impending climate catastrophe. It's a disconnect that grates—to paraphrase Stephen Clark: "are we trying to have 10 Green MPs by the end of the century, or are we saving the planet?" The Green Party will only ever become the political wing of the climate movement if its culture and its own activism become more accommodating to its allies in the broader movement. It needn't be a sacrifice: if the party successfully transforms itself into a relevant political home for all environmentally-minded activists, it will be far better placed to achieve those electoral gains that it's tirelessly targeting.

## Aim for Power

Grossman's third strategic choice is about power. He urges the French Greens to make "the necessary sacrifices" by putting everything "at the service of taking power." This too, seems highly relevant for the Green Party of England and Wales. In fact, the party's strategy is already moving in that direction. Not only through its willingness to enter into electoral pacts with other progressive parties, but also, admirably, through the Ten Bills pledge in its 2019 general election manifesto—a clear statement of intent that tells voters that, yes, a Green Party majority government is not on the cards, but here's how the Green MPs that you help elect will make a difference regardless, immediately.

It's in that vein that the Greens can grow their political influence and what it implicitly acknowledges is that this means working with other parties. In the Westminster context, this especially means coming to an understanding with the Labour party. Much will depend on who Labour chooses to be its next leader: the prospects of fruitful collaboration would have been greatest with a Clive Lewis-led party—for whose daring and visionary leadership fellow Labour MPs weren't ready— but Greens must be prepared to deal with any new leader of the opposition. The concept of a "Green New Deal" appears a potent vehicle for some strategic alignment between progressive opposition parties, and the overall ordeal of a Johnson majority government inflicting Brexit on the country ought to provide a further impetus for pragmatic collaboration.

This will leave some in the Green Party rightly concerned about the party's electoral prospects. Its political profile and relevance will take a substantial hit on the 31st of January, when with the withdrawal of all of the UK's MEPs seven of the ten highest-profile Green Party elected representatives will no longer be elected representatives. With the obvious need for progressive collaboration in Westminster, the party will need to find ways to retain its own voice and to demonstrate its influence. Its electoral strategy must acknowledge and address this challenge—while also embracing the reality that Green influence, power, is found in the party's ability to influence and work with its fellow progressive parties.

## Get the Green Transformation Done

This leaves the Green Party with a big and urgent open question on how it will fight the next general election. Urgent, not because an election is imminent, but because a radical change of course would need to be initiated as soon as possible, for it to have enough of an impact. We're not in a position yet to be able to say in which way the Greens' electoral strategy should change, but to say that it should change is nothing more than stating the obvious. The party must be brave and thorough, and invite a wide range of ideas and suggestions, all of which should be given serious consideration.

Perhaps the Green Party should push to form a united opposition with the other progressive parties and to participate in the next general election as such, provided that electoral reform is in the joint manifesto. Perhaps it should show other progressives the way by inviting them to run joint candidate selection processes. Perhaps, in the event of an unlearning tribal Labour party, the Greens have no choice but to target marginal seats and hurt Labour's prospects there—[as Molly Scott Cato writes]: "We must act with the wisdom to make strategic decisions in the interests of the politics that we represent and no longer allow a failed Labour Party to set the terms of our electoral strategy or ambition."

Perhaps the Green Party should stick with a "coalition of the willing," take Unite to Remain to the next level, and put the climate at the centre of it; "Unite to Remain Alive" anyone? Perhaps the party should accept that its general election campaigns under FPTP are—aside from a handful of constituencies—a wasted effort, and adopt an approach like that of the Women's Equality Party, explicitly seeking to win the arguments rather than the seats.

There will be other options—some more and some less radical than those described here. The point is this: none of them should be rejected out of hand. With a decade of general election stagnation under our belt, despite our collective efforts, we're not in a position to be either cautious or complacent—especially in light of the climate emergency that now requires the exact opposite of a decade of stagnation.

So, let's have the conversations. Let's get to the bottom of the question what it means to be the political wing of the climate movement, and let's bring its activists to the table too. Let's start from the question what our living world needs from our politics and follow that up with the question what our politics then need from the Green Party. Let's not shy away from congratulating ourselves on what we have achieved, but let's also be honest and humble and admit that it's far from enough. Let's get the green transformation done.

> *"The climate movement today is far bigger, better-organized and more active than at the beginning of any previous Democratic president's term."*

# Young People Support Green Politics

*Nick Engelfried*

*In the following viewpoint, Nick Engelfried reports on a youth-led movement that is pressuring the US government to act on climate change. Unfortunately, the author suggests, the fossil fuel industry remains an incredibly powerful and formidable foe, but the fact that these activists are young and invested in the future of the planet is a good sign. Disheartened by the anti-environment policies of the Trump administration, the current climate movement has decided they can no longer sit back and wait for progress to happen. Nick Engelfried is an environmental writer and activist. He currently lives in the Pacific Northwest.*

As you read, consider the following questions:

1. What were the Sunrise Movement protesters calling for?
2. What were the Line 3 pipeline protests?
3. What did some US colleges commit to in 2021?

"As Biden Backslides, a Bigger, Better-Organized Climate Movement Prepares to Seize This 'Now or Never' Moment," by Nick Engelfried, Waging Nonviolence, July 6, 2021, https://wagingnonviolence.org/2021/07/biden-climate-sunrise-movement/. Licensed under CC BY 4.0 International.

Over 500 activists from the youth-led Sunrise Movement descended on Washington, D.C. last week for one of the largest US climate protests since COVID-related restrictions began easing. The young people rallied in front of the White House on June 28, to hear from a range of speakers, including Reps. Jamaal Bowman and Cori Bush, Indigenous pipeline fighters from Anishinaabe land in Minnesota and Sunrise organizers from all corners of the country. All called on President Biden to act swiftly to address the climate crisis.

"I'm from Bethlehem, Pennsylvania, a town built around Bethlehem Steel, a job hub that manufactured steel for infrastructure all over the country," Sunrise activist Mary Collier told the crowd. "But when politicians abandoned my city, all those good-paying jobs vanished."

Amid ongoing talks between the White House and Congress over a national infrastructure bill, Sunrise and other climate groups see an opportunity to attack the climate crisis while rebuilding the economies of blue-collar towns like Bethlehem. However, now that a bipartisan infrastructure bill has been released that contains little in the way of support for clean energy, activists are urging the Biden administration to show it truly is committed to climate action. One of Sunrise's priorities is funding for a Civilian Climate Corps that would employ 1.5 million people in jobs like clean energy construction, sustainable infrastructure and reforestation.

After the recent rally at the White House, Sunrise protesters blockaded all 10 entrances to the building, leading to dozens of arrests. Yet, despite their anger at the president's recent compromises, the young protesters are not anti-Biden. In fact, many volunteered hundreds of hours last year to ensure his election.

"Last fall I spent all my time getting Pennsylvanians out to vote," said Collier, who along with dozens of other youth marched 105 miles from her state's capital in Harrisburg to the White House. "Even after Biden won, I didn't stop—I organized Every Vote Counts actions to defend the vote we had got out for him. We elected Biden with the guarantee that he would create good-paying jobs of the kind I dreamed about, but instead I've seen him compromising with the GOP and negotiating away Bethlehem's future."

## A Once in a Lifetime Opportunity

The Biden administration earned early praise from climate groups soon after taking office in January. On Inauguration Day, Biden rejected the permit for the Keystone XL tar sands pipeline and committed the United States to re-joining the Paris accord. Since then, however, the administration has showed signs of wavering in its commitment to climate justice, refusing to revisit permits for the controversial Line 3 and Dakota Access pipelines. Perhaps most consequentially from a long-term climate perspective, the White House has seemed on the verge of bargaining away commitments to clean energy and zero-emission vehicles originally included in its framework for a national infrastructure bill.

Under pressure from moderate lawmakers like Sen. Joe Manchin of West Virginia, Biden agreed last month to support bipartisan infrastructure legislation that includes almost no major climate policies. Progressive lawmakers are now pushing Democratic leaders to pass a separate bill through the budget process known as reconciliation, which would include support for clean energy, hundreds of thousands of electric vehicle charging stations and other climate priorities. Whether such a bill will eventually move forward remains to be seen. But meanwhile, the administration and Congress face pressure from another source: a climate movement that is tired of waiting for progress as the world burns.

"We have what is potentially a once in a lifetime opportunity to take real action for the climate," said Ivy Jaguzny of Zero Hour, a youth-led climate activist organization founded by high school students. "It's our job to push Biden every single step of the way, because progress isn't going to happen on its own. It's only going to happen if we continue to demand what Biden promised to deliver during his campaign."

# EUROPE'S GREEN WAVE

So can the rag-tag Green movement turn into a veritable political force, the social democracy of the 21st century? That's unlikely to happen overnight. They don't yet have a loyal base that can compare with industrial workers and trade unions. Green parties are popular with urban educated public-sector workers and often loud on lifestyle issues like cycling and recycling, but quiet on social policies, education, security and other important questions of government. They can even be anti-science on issues like vaccinations, homeopathy and nuclear power. It might be hard for them to get rid of these silly beliefs without alienating their core supporters.

The climate movement today is far bigger, better-organized and more active than at the beginning of any previous Democratic president's term. And while COVID largely prevented activists from organizing large in-person protests in the first few months of Biden's administration, that is changing as virus-related restrictions related to travel and gatherings ease. Now, climate activists are shaping the public narrative in ways they have often struggled to do in the past.

"Democratic House members joined protesters from the left-leaning Sunrise Movement outside the White House to demand that far-reaching climate policies be added to the [infrastructure] package," read a recent *Washington Post* article that included a photo of Sunrise activists marching behind the banner "Biden: No Compromises, No Excuses." This is as an example of how high-profile protest tactics are allowing climate organizers to set the terms of the conversation on Capitol Hill with an authority they have rarely enjoyed. During former President Obama's first year in office, for example, progressive activist voices were often drowned out by the more vocal, attention-garnering Tea Party.

In fact, it was not until a couple of years into Obama's first term in office that the former president faced large-scale direct

> But even if they don't end up heading national governments anytime soon, Greens can make cities more livable and push parties to their left and right towards properly facing the greatest challenge of this century, global warming. President Macron's response the day after the elections proves this.
>
> It also shows that the planet wins when Greens govern, or when their rivals are forced to adopt once-Green ideas. The Greens are growing, and though they might never be dominant, they can be a vital force in the politics of the future.
>
> "Opinion: A European Green Wave May Be Coming—Finally," by James Jackson, DW, May 7, 2020.

action protests focused on climate issues. In contrast, less than six months into Biden's presidency, the climate movement has not only blockaded the White House, it has taken its demands to key Congressional districts all over the country.

## A Growing Nationwide Movement

"We have walked 266 miles to get here," said Sunrise activist Ema Govea, standing at the base of the Golden Gate Bridge last month. Govea and roughly 100 other Sunrise members had just marched from Paradise, California—a town demolished by wildfires in 2018—to San Francisco, where they rallied outside the homes of House Speaker Nancy Pelosi and Sen. Diane Feinstein. "This is not the end," Govea added. "This march will reignite a movement, and this is just the beginning."

The march from Paradise to San Francisco was one of three similar treks recently organized by Sunrise in the lead-up to last week's White House action. In the South, activists marched 400 miles from New Orleans to Houston, where they ended their journey with a sit-in at Sen. Ted Cruz's home. In Pennsylvania, marchers like Collier walked all the way to the White House itself.

The young people involved show how climate groups are using creative tactics and direct action to bring their demands not only to Washington, D.C. but also the home states of key members of Congress.

As a next step, Sunrise—which is organized into local chapters or "hubs" scattered all over the United States—is calling for a nationwide day of action in support of the Civilian Conservation Corps, to be held on July 15. This strategy of combining large, high-profile protests in the nation's capital with more distributed actions that pressure individual members of Congress is one Sunrise has used successfully before, including in late 2018 when the organization helped put the idea of a Green New Deal at the center of Congressional Democrats' agenda. However, Sunrise Movement is only one among many climate groups now organizing for federal action in far-flung parts of the country.

Other than the infrastructure package, probably no climate-related issue has garnered more attention from national groups this year than the Line 3 pipeline, a conduit for tar sands oil from Canada. In early June, thousands of people converged on Minnesota for days of Indigenous-led protests against the pipeline, which culminated in a direct action that temporarily stopped work on a pump station. Hundreds joined a semi-permanent encampment in the pipeline's path, and the protests show no signs of dying down.

On June 30, Rising Tide North America held a virtual direct action training to prepare people to join the growing movement against Line 3. An email to supporters said the training would cover "principles of direct action … what to take to an action and how to plan an action," as well as "what you need to know about coming to support the frontlines" on Anishinaabe land. All this is indicative of a climate movement emerging from the COVID pandemic more coordinated at a national level than perhaps ever before, as well as one that has learned over the past year to use online tools like Zoom to maximum effect.

Much of this movement's energy post-COVID has gone into pressuring Congress and the Biden administration to take action, whether by passing a strong infrastructure bill or stopping fossil fuel projects like Line 3. At the same time, other activist groups are pursuing another strategy they have become increasingly adept at: strategically confronting the political and economic power of fossil fuel industries themselves.

## Shaping the Narrative to Win

On June 16, Maine Gov. Janet Mills signed into law a bill making the state the first to adopt legislation requiring its public employee pension funds and state treasury system to divest from fossil fuels. It was a momentous occasion for climate activists fighting to win progress at the state and local levels that could help build momentum for federal action.

"It's a good time for the climate movement to have a win, especially one as concrete as this," said Anna Siegel of Maine Youth for Climate, one of the organizations that pushed for the divestment bill. "These are victories that help move us forward into a world that puts people and planet over the profits of corporations."

In fact, 2021 has seen a string of successes for the fossil fuel divestment movement. According to Divest Ed, which works with student activists on college divestment campaigns, at least 10 US higher education institutions have unveiled new divestment commitments so far this year. They include University of Michigan, Princeton, Columbia College and University of Southern California. Each announcement, like the statewide divestment campaign in Maine, targets the fossil fuel industry's public image and contributes to a larger public narrative against which debates over federal legislative and regulatory action take place.

There can be no denying climate groups have a long way to go before they can expect to push federal climate legislation over the finish line, if such a victory occurs at all during Biden's crucial first year in office. The fossil fuel industry also still has plenty of political clout, as evidenced by a recent undercover video recorded by Greenpeace, which shows an Exxon Mobil lobbyist bragging about the company's efforts to kill climate provisions in the infrastructure package. Even so, grassroots activists are shaping how media and political figures talk about climate in ways that would have been hard to imagine even a few years ago.

"We're not just marching in the streets, although we're doing that," Zero Hour's Jaguzny said. "We're lobbying and advocating for meaningful climate actions on the Hill. We're trying to keep oil in the ground. We're trying to build clean energy and public transit for everyone and facilitate a just transition. This is the time for action—it's now or never."

| "In fact, the US has a long history of
radical alternative-party ideas."

# We Need More Radical Parties

*Scott McLarty*

*In the following viewpoint, Scott McLarty explores why in the United States, politics is dominated by the Republican and Democratic Parties. The author notes that the system is entirely stacked against third-party candidates. It is difficult if not nearly impossible for third-party candidates to get on the ballot in most states. They are usually kept out of presidential debates. Yet additional political parties would benefit the country, the author suggests: ideas initially seen as "radical" have become part of our national values. At the time of this writing, Scott McLarty was media coordinator for the US Green Party.*

As you read, consider the following questions:

1. What is ranked choice voting?
2. How does the Commission on Presidential Debates (CPD) help keep the Republican and Democratic Parties in power, according to the author?
3. According to the viewpoint, how do "radical" parties and policies tend to change a country's values over time?

"The Green Party's Radical Common Sense," by Scott McLarty, Truthdig, October 28, 2016. Orginally published on Truthdig. https://www.truthdig.com/articles/the-green-partys-radical-common-sense/. Reprinted by permission.

G ermany and other European countries have a thriving
multiparty political culture. The US used to have one too.
In 1916, five parties were seated in Congress.

In his *Washington Post* article "In Europe, the Green Party is
a force. In the US, it's irrelevant. Here's why," Per Urlaub, associate
professor of German studies at the University of Texas, contends
that "the American electoral system is heavily weighted against
small political parties."

He's right. Alternative parties must wrestle with ballot-access
laws, enacted since 1916 by Democratic and Republican legislators
in many states, that privilege major-party candidates and hinder
others. In some states, alternative parties are effectively banned
from participation.

When alternative parties do get on the ballot, their candidates
often face the "spoiler" accusation. The supposed spoiler effect
can be eliminated by replacing the prevailing "first past the
post" system with "ranked choice," which allows people to rank
their preferences.

Reforms like ranked choice voting (RCV) and proportional
representation—which gave Germany and other European
countries their multiparty legislatures—are considered radical here,
even though they grant voters greater power and more options.

Greens have urged such reforms for years, but Democrats and
Republicans prefer to maintain their exclusive hold. A chance for
RCV in California died in early October with Democratic Gov.
Jerry Brown's veto.

The major parties solidified their grip in 1988, when the
Commission on Presidential Debates (CPD) seized control of
the debates from the League of Women Voters. Contrary to its
"nonpartisan" label, the CPD is run by Democratic and Republican
representatives for the benefit of their own candidates. The League
has called the CPD debates a "fraud on the American voter."

The CPD adopted its poll-based criteria to determine
participation in the debates after the 1998 gubernatorial election
in Minnesota. Independent candidate Jesse Ventura was dismissed

as "not viable," with a tiny percentage in the polls until he was allowed to participate in a debate. His poll numbers shot up and he went on to win.

When the CPD witnessed what happened in Minnesota, it raised the requirement to 15 percent in the polls in 2000 to spare Al Gore and George W. Bush from facing Ralph Nader and Pat Buchanan in the debates.

The CPD's rules aren't meant to bar "unviable" candidates, they're designed to keep alternative-party candidates from becoming viable.

There's nothing inevitable about having only two parties. We don't have a two-party system, we have a two-party racket.

Voters are aware they've been cheated. Their frustration is evident in polls showing they favor more options than two on Election Day, and the high disapproval ratings for Donald Trump and Hillary Clinton.

## Radical? Only in the US

Per Urlaub's main complaint about the US Green Party is its "radicalism." In fact, the US has a long history of radical alternative-party ideas.

Abolition of slavery, women's suffrage, the eight-hour workday, worker benefits, public schools, unemployment compensation, the minimum wage, child labor laws, direct election of senators, Social Security, civil rights for blacks and other disenfranchised peoples—all were first represented in the electoral forum by alternative parties.

Marginalization of minor parties in the late 20th century is an unmentioned reason for the shift to the right in both major parties and the disappearance of big progressive ideas.

Obamacare isn't a big progressive idea. It's a repackaging of the conservative Heritage Foundation's individual mandate proposal and RomneyCare, implemented by then-governor Mitt Romney, a Republican, from Massachusetts. It was drafted by Democrats with the participation of insurance-industry representatives.

Greens support a single-payer health care program, so that Americans can have the guaranteed medical care enjoyed by citizens of every other democratic developed nation. Only in the US is universal health care dismissed as radical and unrealistic.

Urlaub never mentions what makes the US Green Party radical. He does, however, cite projects for conversion to clean, renewable energy that are implemented in Europe and advocated by presidential nominee Jill Stein and other Green candidates in the "Green New Deal," which aims for freedom from fossil fuels by 2030.

Global warming was nearly absent from the three Clinton-Trump debates, even after Hurricane Matthew pounded Haiti and the Southern states.

Young people will live with the consequences of rule by two parties awash in corporate money and influence. Millennials face an era of deteriorating quality of life, increasing personal debt, exported jobs, eroded rights and freedoms, lawless militarism, and social breakdown as the planet heats up. Urlaub advises us that "climate change, dwindling energy resources and growing human and economic costs from natural disasters will do more to promote ecological consciousness and political change in mainstream America than the radical rhetoric of the Green Party."

Greens say we can't wait for the severest effects of global warming before taking action to prevent them—and changing the political landscape to enable such action.

As with the climate crisis, radical measures are often exactly what we need.

In 2004, Green Mayor Jason West of New Paltz, N.Y., inspired by the Green Party's support for LGBT equality, solemnized the weddings of same-sex couples—and was prosecuted. Nine years later, Hillary Clinton joined the rest of the civilized world and endorsed same-sex marriage.

In Richmond, Calif., Green Mayor Gayle McLaughlin used eminent domain to keep residents with underwater mortgages in their homes. McLaughlin infuriated the foreclosing banks—

whose predatory lending and trading in toxic securities crashed the economy in 2008.

What Urlaub calls radicalism is progressive leadership. Greens know very well that compromise and collaboration are often necessary in public office, but one doesn't march into battle armed with capitulations.

The Green New Deal is a vision in the tradition of President Franklin Roosevelt's New Deal and President Johnson's Great Society. The Democratic Party has abandoned such visions, especially since the Clintons led it to the right in the early 1990s.

Donald Trump's vision for America is frightening. Hillary Clinton's vision is "I'm not Trump." She doesn't even bother to promise hope or change. The Green Party says we can do better.

# Periodical and Internet Sources Bibliography

*The following articles have been selected to supplement the diverse views presented in this chapter.*

Ballotpedia, "Green Party," https://ballotpedia.org/Green_Party

Evan Blake, "Howie Hawkins and the Green Party: Capitalist Politics in the Guise of 'Ecosocialism,'" World Socialist Web Site, May 29, 2020. https://www.wsws.org/en/articles/2020/05/29/gree-m29 .html

James Jay Carafano and Jack Spencer, "Protecting the Planet While Great Powers Compete," The Heritage Foundation, January 11, 2021. https://www.heritage.org/environment/commentary /protecting-the-planet-while-great-powers-compete

*Environmental Politics Journal.* https://www.tandfonline.com/toc /fenp20/current

*Global Environmental Politics*, MIT Press Direct. https://direct.mit .edu/glep

Green Party of the United States, "Ten Key Values." https://www .gp.org/ten_key_values

Ezra Klein, "What If American Democracy Fails the Climate Crisis?" *New York Times Magazine*, June 22, 2021. https://www.nytimes .com/2021/06/22/magazine/ezra-klein-climate-crisis.html

Robinson Meyer, "The Millennial Era of Climate Politics Has Arrived," *The Atlantic*, February 7, 2019. https://www.theatlantic .com/science/archive/2019/02/aocgreen-new-deal-new-era -millennial-climate-politics/582295/

New Brunswick Green Party, "Green Accomplishments." https:// greennbvert.ca/green-party-accomplishments/

Shirelle Phelps and Jeffrey Lehman, ed., "The History of the Green Party," *West's Encyclopedia of American Law*, June 10, 2015. https://usapoliticaldatabase.weebly.com/history-of-the-green -party.html

John Rensenbrink, "Challenge and Response," Green Party of the United States, February 2003. https://www.gp.org/challenge_and_ response

John Rensenbrink, "Early History of the United States Green Party," Green Party of the United States, May 15, 2017. https://www.gp.org/early_history

Barry Seppard, "United States: Democrats Move to Suppress Green Party Vote," Green Left, September 29, 2020. https://www.greenleft.org.au/content/united-states-democrats-move-suppress-green-party-vote

Yasmeen Serhan, "The Far-Right View on Climate Politics," *The Atlantic*, August 10, 2021. https://www.theatlantic.com/international/archive/2021/08/far-right-view-climate-ipcc/619709/

Per Urlaub, "Why Can't the US Green Party Get Traction?" *Houston Chronicle*, October 18, 2016. https://www.houstonchronicle.com/local/gray-matters/article/Why-is-the-U-S-Green-Party-so-irrelevant-9980515.php

OPPOSING
VIEWPOINTS®
SERIES

# CHAPTER 2

# Where Do Green Politics Fit into the Political Spectrum?

# Chapter Preface

On the political spectrum, the Green Party sits left of the Democrats. In politics, "left" refers to liberals, people who support ideas such as equality, equal rights, and progress. They typically support progressive reforms, those designed to create greater social and economic equality.

People on the "right" are more conservative, supporting the current systems and institutions. They back ideas such as the rule of authority, hierarchy, order, duty, and tradition. The political spectrum was divided into left and right after the French Revolution. In the 1789 French National Assembly, the nobility and high-ranking religious leaders were seated to the speaker's right. Commoners and less powerful clergy were seated to the left. Thus, the right-hand side became associated with pro-aristocracy views. The left-hand side became associated with more radical views supportive of the middle class.

People who consider themselves progressives generally have views to the left of Democrats. Progressives attack the extreme concentration of wealth among a tiny number of people. They argue that opportunities are not equally available in the US. They try to put more power in the hands of workers instead of big businesses.

Progressive politics have been around for well over a century. In fact, the progressive movement was most powerful in the first two decades of the twentieth century. However, the Republican and Democratic Parties developed a stranglehold on power that made it difficult for any other party to win major elections. Other political parties have tried and failed to make a difference in national politics.

Political parties do not stay the same over the years. They may shift more left or right, or they may shift more to the center. Within a party, people may be more to the center or to an extreme. People who have always supported one party may discover they no longer agree with that party's ideals. Some progressive voters feel the Green Party better supports their views.

In some countries, particularly in Europe, Green Party candidates have won enough votes to hold positions in the national government. The Green Party has done best in countries where the environment was a matter of national discussion. When other parties discuss environmental issues, more people pay attention. Green Party voters tend to be younger. They also tend to have jobs, so they are not as concerned about unemployment. This allows more emotional space to be focused on the environment.

However, in the US, the two-party system dominates. Many people believe their vote counts for more if they stay in one of the major parties. Some even feel that the Green Party is not that different from the Democratic Party. In fact, the Democratic Party has adopted many policies originally developed by the Greens. Green party politicians may see that as their true value: they can push the Democrats to the left.

Many Americans want to see more environmental protection. But they don't believe the Green Party has enough power to win elections. The following chapter explores how the Green Party and green politics fit into US and international politics.

| "Greens put the common good before corporate greed, and the public interest before private profit."

# Greens Support Social Justice

*Peter Tatchell*

*In the following viewpoint, Peter Tatchell explains why he left Great Britain's Labour Party. Tatchell feels Labour once supported socialism (a system where the workers own the means of production, such as factories) and democracy (government by the people). However, in his view, the Labour Party no longer supports social justice and human rights for all. Instead, he sees the Green Party as more progressive, supporting economic and social equality. The author argues that people who are politically to the left, supporting progressive ideas, should vote Green. Peter Tatchell is a British human rights campaigner, known for his work with LGBTQ social movements.*

As you read, consider the following questions:

1. In the author's view, what has changed in Britain's Labour Party?
2. How are environmental issues and social justice linked, according to the author?
3. Why does the author think people should vote for the Green Party rather than smaller left-wing parties?

"Why I Joined the Greens," by Peter Tatchell, Green Party. Reprinted by permission.

R adical socialists in England and Wales face a dilemma. The Labour Party is now beyond reform. The idea of recapturing Labour for the left is a hopeless dream.

Equally depressing, alternative left parties like the Socialist Alliance and Respect offer little cause for optimism. The Socialist Alliance tried, but failed, to secure electoral success. Respect is neither grassroots nor democratic. It is run on the same "democratic centralist" lines as the Blairite Labour Party. All major decisions are taken at the top. It is dominated by the Socialist Workers Party, which is notorious for packing meetings and organising secret slates to secure the election of its people to key positions.

I left the Labour Party in 2000, after 22 years membership. My reason? "New" Labour has abandoned both socialism and democracy. It is no longer committed to the redistribution of wealth and power. Tony Blair spends more time with millionaire businessmen than trade union leaders. The gap between rich and poor has widened since 1997. Civil liberties are under ceaseless attack by David Blunkett, the most right-wing home secretary since Sir David Maxwell Fyfe in the 1950s.

There is, alas, no possibility of undoing Blair's right-wing "coup." Internal party democracy has been extinguished. Ordinary members have no say. Everything important is decided by The Dear Leader and his acolytes. Fixing the selection process for the London mayoral candidate in 2000 to defeat Ken Livingstone was one of many examples of Labour's corruption. No socialist can remain in a party that rigs ballots and denies members a meaningful say in the decisions of their party.

I joined Labour because I want social justice and human rights for all. My values and aspirations remain the same. Labour's have changed fundamentally and irreversibly. Winning back Labour to socialism and democracy is now impossible.

No political party lasts forever. Even the most progressive party eventually decays or turns reactionary. Labour's great, historic achievement was the creation of the welfare state. The current party leadership is in the process of privatising it.

Leaving Labour does not mean giving up the battle for a fair and just society. There is an alternative option. After two decades of moving from right to left, the Green Party now occupies the progressive political space once held by left-wing Labour. It offers the most credible left alternative to Labour's pro-war, pro-big business and pro-Bush policies.

The Green Party's manifesto for a sustainable society incorporates key socialist values. It rejects privatisation, free market economics and globalisation, and includes commitments to public ownership, worker's rights, economic democracy, progressive taxation and the redistribution of wealth and power.

Greens put the common good before corporate greed, and the public interest before private profit. Forging a red-green synthesis, they integrate policies for social justice with policies for tackling the life-threatening dangers posed by global warming, environmental pollution, resource depletion and species extinction.

Unlike the traditional left, with its superficial environmentalism, Greens understand there is no point campaigning for social justice if we don't have a habitable planet. Ecological sustainability is the precondition for a just society. The Greens also recognise that tackling the global ecological threat requires constraints on the power of big corporations. Profiteering and free trade has to be subordinated to policies for the survival of humanity. Can any socialist disagree with that?

Although the Green Party is not perfect (is any party perfect?), its anti-capitalist agenda gives practical expression to socialist ideas. Very importantly, ordinary members are empowered to decide policy. The Greens are a grassroots democratic party, where activism is encouraged and where members with ideals and principles are valued.

Unlike tiny left parties, such as the Socialist Alliance and Respect, Greens have a proven record of success at the ballot box, with candidates elected in the London, Scottish, local and European elections. These elected Greens are a force for social progress, far to the left of Labour on all issues. They are also well to the left of the Socialist Alliance and Respect on questions like women's and gay rights, health care, animal welfare, the environment and third world development.

People tempted to support Respect in the forthcoming elections need to answer two crucial questions. Why split the left-wing vote and thereby diminish the electoral prospects of both Respect and the Green Party? Why vote for an unproven political force like Respect when there is a credible and radical left party—the Greens—that already has seats and can win lots more with the support of people on the left?

> *"The Greens dress up in radical clothing but offer little more than class collaboration and empty reforms."*

# The Green Party Isn't Far Enough Left

*Ezra Brain*

*In the following viewpoint, Ezra Brain notes that many voters were looking for a more progressive candidate in the 2020 election. The Green Party candidate, Howie Hawkins, offered an alternative to the Democratic and Republican candidates. However, the viewpoint author argues that the Green Party is not as revolutionary as it claims. The US Green Party is willing to work within the current capitalist system, in which wealthy individuals run businesses for profit. In this author's view, that does not go far enough to support workers' rights. Ezra Brain is a genderqueer writer, activist, and teacher.*

As you read, consider the following questions:

1. Why did the author think many voters were looking for alternatives to the major candidates in the 2020 election?
2. Why does the author think it's dangerous to collaborate with capitalists?
3. Why does the author think America needs a workers' party?

"A Socialist Case Against Howie Hawkins and the Green Party," by Ezra Brain, Left Voice, September 22, 2020. Reprinted by permission.

A s the 2020 election draws ever closer, a sector of voters is looking for an alternative to the two main parties. Joe Biden and Donald Trump represent some of the most depraved elements of American capitalism and, in the midst of the largest uprising against racist violence in US history, both have a horrific record of racism. Millions of voters—including some of the organized Left—are searching for a candidate who better represents their politics. This rejection of lesser evilism is progressive and shows that the current moment has pushed many to the left. Many are being drawn to Howie Hawkins and the Green Party.

Hawkins, the Green Party candidate for president, is an appealing figure: he's a life-long organizer, former UPS worker, Teamster, and committed leftist. The Green Party, which received around 1.5 million votes in 2016, formally adopted the label "eco-socialist" at its 2016 National Convention. Hawkins, like all other third-party candidates, is being shut out at every turn by an undemocratic system of elections designed to keep only the two bourgeois parties in power. This has led many socialists to support Hawkins and the Green Party in the belief that he is either a socialist or that a vote for the Green Party is a way to challenge the capitalist system. However, the task for socialists in this election cycle is not to fight against the lesser evil by allying with capitalists as the Green Party's strategy does, but by providing a perspective of how socialists should engage in elections.

## A Multi-Class Party Advocating "Eco-Socialism"

While much of their rhetoric is certainly appealing, it is important to understand that the Green Party is far from a revolutionary, socialist, or even a workers' party. It is a multi-class party that operates on the principle that it is possible to reconcile the conflicting interests of the working class and the capitalist class. So while the party's platform talks about the need to wrest power from the hands of the greedy one percent, the party also nominated Ralph Nader, a millionaire and a union-buster, as its 1996 and 2000 presidential candidate. But history shows that multi-class parties, no matter their origins, always come to be dominated by their bourgeois elements through the capitalists who they allow in their ranks. While Hawkins is certainly to the left of both Nader and Jill Stein, the 2016 Green Party candidate, his name on the ticket doesn't change the nature of the party itself.

Because the Green Party is organized around an "issue"—the environment—rather than a class, it has allowed capitalists into their ranks and they are in control of the party. To see this we only have to look at the contradiction between the websites of Hawkins and the platform of the Green Party itself. Hawkins is the only candidate with widespread ballot access to have the Green New Deal as part of his platform and his own website states, "Implementing the Green New Deal will require eco-socialism—social ownership in key sectors in order to democratically plan the coordinated reconstruction of all economic sectors for ecological sustainability." But the Green Party's official website immediately gives the lie to this "eco-socialism" concept: "Business leaders, advertising agencies and even Hollywood must be enlisted [to help fight climate change], a quid pro quo for government bail out of banks and corporations."

In other words, the Green Party is perfectly happy to give government bailouts to banks and corporations as long as they aid the fight against climate change—as if capitalists could ever actually fight against climate change. This is damning, considering that socialists should be fighting for nationalization of these same banks and putting corporations under workers' control, not writing checks to capitalists. The Green Party, however, is perfectly happy to maintain the system of capitalism and collaborate actively with banks and corporations. The Greens support private ownership of the means of production, but with a few more regulations. That isn't socialist—it's nothing more than an attempt to reform capitalism.

Collaborating with capital is as disastrous in the fight against climate change as it is in the fight for socialism. The nature of capitalism is that it must always expand and generate greater profit. To do that, businesses need to continue exploiting both labor and natural resources. There is no such thing as "sustainable capitalism"—just as there is no such thing as an "eco-socialism" that exists hand in hand with banks and corporations.

Socialism means workers' control of the means of production through a workers' state, as a step toward the disappearance of all social classes. Under a socialist system, the environment would be protected by the power of workers' democratic planning of the economy. Protecting the environment and creating an ecologically sustainable economy would be an inherent part of a socialist economic system. That the Green Party is using the abstract and ill-defined concept of "eco-socialism" as a slogan while also proposing active collaboration with capitalists shows the utter bankruptcy of its strategy. The Greens dress up in radical clothing but offer little more than class collaboration and empty reforms. At the end of the day, the Green Party believes in an economy that is neither capitalist nor socialist but rather "eco-socialist"—which, in practice, appears to look like a watered-down version of European social democracy where capitalists can continue to exploit both workers and the environment, but in a more "sustainable" way—but at the end of the day, capitalist productive and social relations remain in place.

Socialism is more than just nationalized industry, which is undoubtedly what Hawkins is implying when he says "social ownership in key sectors." Many countries have nationalized industries, but that doesn't make them socialist—the state is still controlled by the bourgeoisie. Simply substituting bosses with government bureaucrats doesn't change the class relationships within the economy. Socialists should be calling for the nationalization of industries under workers' control, which would ensure that newly state-owned businesses are run by the workers to meet the needs of society, not to maximize profits. Hawkins's failure to call for this shows the limitations of fighting for the politics of "socialism" within a multi-class framework: The capitalists in the party will water down the platform until it is just minor reforms that don't challenge capitalism as an economic system.

## Electoralism Alone Is Not Enough

The limitations of the Green Party's politics can be seen throughout its platform. Some of its proposals (such as creating a National Health Service) are relatively radical, while others (such as the proposal to "curb corporate power" by "re-design[ing] corporations to serve our society, democracy and the environment") put forward the dangerous illusion that corporations can serve the public good. Taken as a whole, even though they bring up some reforms that would benefit the working class, their platform makes it very clear the Greens are about reforming capitalism, not defeating it. None of the party's policies actually challenge capitalism as a system.

Socialists must fight for every reform that will benefit workers and the oppressed. But we know that capitalists will reverse whatever reforms we win at the first opportunity. Real change cannot be won through elections—We win real concessions by protesting in the streets and challenging the capitalists' control of the means of production. Electoral campaigns—especially those at the national level—can amplify those fights, but we must formulate every struggle for reforms as part of a larger strategy to build up the power of the working class and topple capitalism.

Our goal must always be to further the fight for socialism, which means building a working-class force powerful enough to overthrow the capitalist state. Participating in elections can be an important tactic to help build that force, but we have to resist the pull of electoralism as a strategy. History is littered with the carcasses of parties that tried to win socialism at the ballot box. It is a strategy that leads only to disaster.

When we use elections, it should be to rally support for revolution. We have to be clear-eyed about how to use elections to advance the building of a truly revolutionary party—one based in the working class and that actively prepares for the moment of revolution, not that collaborates with capitalists for "eco-socialism."

# AN ANTI-GREEN PERSPECTIVE

The Greens are no better on domestic climate policy. Their manifesto revels in the opportunity of using decarbonisation as a tool for social change, redesigning our cities, houses and transport systems to suit their vision of a socially inclusive future. Solutions that would not require fundamental changes in how we live and run large chunks of the economy, such as carbon capture or the nuclear option, are either ignored or ruled out.

The environment will not be a serious issue in this election. But for those that do care about it, this election is an opportunity for a serious debate about environmental policy. It is time to break the link, beloved of Europe's Greens, between environmental protection and progressive social policy. Insisting that we have to reform capitalism before we can save the planet is clearly a good idea if your priority is reforming capitalism, but a very bad idea if you want to persuade China to help save the planet.

I fear that many people will be voting Green because they want to send a message of concern about climate change. How many realise that they will be voting for a party that places the environment relatively low in its policy priorities, and whose political agenda has become part of the problem, not part of the solution? No one who really cares about the environment should consider voting for a party that is prepared to hold the planet hostage to its social justice agenda.

"Why I Won't Be Voting Green," by Myles Allen, *The Guardian*, April 15, 2010.

## The Greens Are Also a Dead-End for Socialists

In an article in *Tempest*, Ashley Smith and Charlie Post argue that: "Clearly, socialists need to contest elections when we can with candidates of our own and on our own ballot line. That's why we advocate voting for Howie Hawkins, despite the problems of the Green Party, as a protest vote and alternative to the dead end of lesser evilism."

This quote is revealing because it shows the way that many socialists who recognize that the Green Party is a multi-class party and not socialist are rationalizing their support for Hawkins. They argue, like *Jacobin* editor Bhaskar Sunkara, that we should vote for Hawkins as a protest of the Democrats but not build the Green Party as an institution. What is most interesting about this line of reasoning is that, despite being employed as an argument against lesser evilism, it features a very similar logic.

Lesser evilism proposes that we support a candidate who is in direct opposition to our politics (Joe Biden) to resist a candidate who is even more opposed to our politics (Dondald Trump). The issues with this are numerous—many of which are outlined in Smith and Post's article. But this is the same logic that is being employed with calling to support the Greens.

The argument goes that socialists should support the Greens—even though their platform calls for the continuation of capitalism—in order to protest a more right-wing capitalist party. This will demonstrate that the public has lost support for the Democrats which will, so the theory goes, facilitate the creation of a left-wing third party strong enough to take-on the Democrats and Republicans.

But the contradictions with this position make it untenable for socialists. First, while of course Hawkins is to the left of Biden, the Green Party does not help the working class in the fight for socialism because it calls for the continuation of capitalism. In addition, the Green Party doesn't play a role in advancing class struggle. They were absent from the Black Lives Matter movement that brought millions to the streets and they didn't do any workplace organizing during the pandemic. They aren't a part of class struggle and they don't advance class consciousness in workers because the Greens aren't asking people to vote for a workers' party but, rather, a multi-class one. This not only ignores the centrality of the working class but also continues the illusion that class conciliation is possible. Additionally, as we have seen internationally, if they actually got elected the Greens would ultimately be just as devastating for working people as any other neo-reformist party.

In addition, it isn't possible to both call for a vote for the Greens while also trying to work against them. We are in a moment of deep capitalist crisis, with millions having just taken the streets and millions more suffering under both the pandemic and the economic crisis. Now is the time when socialists must be clear about what exactly we support. The many tweets earlier this year about a #DemExit show that people are losing faith in the Democratic Party. The fact that the Green Party draws millions of voters each election cycle illustrates that there is a public appetite for a left-wing party. Support for socialism among young people is the highest it has been in generations and socialists have to be both specific and strategic about how we build in the current moment.

A vote for the Greens presents to them as an acceptable alternative to the two main parties of capital. Rather than doing the preparatory work necessary to build a socialist party of the working class, these socialists are calling for a vote for a party that supports capitalism.

This is why, at the end of the day, the argument to vote for the Greens has too many similarities with lesser evilism to ignore. This strategy seems to argue that throwing our support behind a capitalist party (even one that calls itself "eco-socialist") can work out in our favor because it will allow for more favorable conditions to organize in. But in reality, it confuses the role elections can play in generating support for socialist ideas and obfuscates socialists' vision for change on a mass scale. It is vital that socialists be intransigent with our political independence, especially in times of crisis, so that we never betray the working class by supporting our oppressors. This strategy compromises our principles in the hope that it will somehow benefit us, despite there being no evidence to prove that will occur.

The Green Party reveals the limits of calling for a third party in the abstract. While it is certainly true that the Democratic Party is a dead end for socialists, that does not mean that voting for just any party that is "independent" of the Democrats or the Republicans advances socialism. Voting for the Green Party is just another way for socialists to exempt themselves from elections.

## For a Workers' Party That Fights for Socialism

Socialists should support the democratic right of the Green Party to run in elections, get ballot access, and participate in debates. But socialists should not support voting for Hawkins and the Green Party as a means of fighting for socialism or against the Democrats and Republicans. The reasons are overwhelming. The party and its candidate are in bed with the capitalists because the Green Party is a multi-class party. It can never stand for overthrowing capitalism or establishing a workers' state. Instead, Hawkins and the Greens propose to nationalize a few industries, enact some reforms, and create partnerships with corporations to fight climate change. This is an insufficient platform from a multi-class party with an inherently electoralist strategy.

It's not enough simply to be to the left of the Democratic Party. We need a workers' party that fights for socialism and against imperialism. We need a party that understands the limitations of elections and how to use them. We need a party that fights for reforms as part of a larger strategy to overthrow the capitalist state, not as an end in themselves. And we need to start to build that party now.

The Green Party is not the party we need and as a multi-class organization it will never become that party—though some left sectors of the Green Party could split from the party and help build a revolutionary organization. We're in the midst of a pandemic, the worst economic crisis in decades, a climate crisis, and an advance from the right wing. We don't have time to sit around and wait for this party to be created, we need to take up the preparatory tasks now. Because the right wing is advancing now and the only way to fight back against it is through class struggle and an organized left. We can't waste our energies on multi-class parties in the vain hope that it'll shake out in our favor. Now is the time to begin to organize a revolutionary party.

> *"Were Hawkins or any other Green
> Party politician to come to power
> in the US, their nationalist outlook
> would compel them to enforce the
> dictates of the American financial
> oligarchy, including through policies
> of war and austerity."*

# Greens Are Just Democrats in Disguise

*Evan Blake*

*In the following viewpoint, Evan Blake argues that in the United States, the Green Party is not really very different from the Democratic Party. The author claims that the Green Party is mainly interested in making sure Democrats win elections. Greens hope that by entering the conversation, they will be able to push Democrats further left. But will the Democratic candidates fulfill those promises once they are elected? The Green Party pushes some progressive ideals, but in this author's view, it is not nearly far enough to the left. He claims that internationally, Greens abandon their principles when they gain power. Evan Blake writes for World Socialist Web Site, a socialist news site.*

"Howie Hawkins and the Green Party: Capitalist Politics in the Guise of 'Ecosocialism,'" by Evan Blake, World Socialist Web Site, May 29, 2020. Reprinted by permission.

As you read, consider the following questions:

1. Did the Hawkins-Walker campaign plan to challenge the capitalist system, according to the viewpoint?
2. Why does this author believe the Green Party is not truly a party of the working class?
3. What political movement does this author think people should support?

In the aftermath of Bernie Sanders' endorsement of Democratic Party candidate Joe Biden last month, the Green Party is presenting itself as the continuation of Sanders' "political revolution." Workers and youth seeking an alternative to the Democrats and Republicans must be warned: The Green Party is a capitalist party with no real independence from the Democrats.

The Green Party is presently on track to nominate Howie Hawkins, one of the co-founders of the party in 1984, as its presidential candidate. Hawkins has announced that Angela Walker will be his running mate for vice president. Both Hawkins and Walker are also members of Socialist Party USA and Solidarity, pseudo-left groups that operate in the orbit of the Democratic Party.

The Hawkins-Walker campaign platform itself is an eclectic list of various reform proposals, centered on an "Ecosocialist Green New Deal." To fund their programs, they call not for the expropriation of the wealth of the capitalists or the nationalization of any corporations, but simply "progressive taxation." The words "working class," "capitalist class" and "revolution" do not appear in their platform.

The various reforms proposed by the Greens, however, are no more meaningful than those proposed by Sanders, Alexandria Ocasio-Cortez and the like, as they are tied to a political strategy aimed at bolstering the Democratic Party, a party of Wall Street and the military.

Under conditions of the COVID-19 pandemic, in which over 350,000 people have died worldwide, including over 100,000 Americans, while the working class faces social dislocation on a scale not seen since the Great Depression and is being forced to return to work in deadly conditions, the response of the Hawkins-Walker campaign and the Green Party is to try to keep opposition contained within the framework of bourgeois politics.

Their campaign has only released a handful of statements addressing the pandemic, none of which raise any serious solutions to this unprecedented crisis. Rather, they call on Congress to expand Medicare and enact the Green New Deal, urge Trump to utilize the Defense Production Act more thoroughly, plead for the Occupational Safety and Health Administration to demand that personal protective equipment be provided to workers, and place other minor demands on the existing political establishment.

All of their statements omit any criticisms of the nearly unanimous Democratic Party vote—including by Sanders and Elizabeth Warren—for the multi-trillion-dollar handout to Wall Street through the CARES Act. Further, they say nothing of the culpability of Democratic governors across the US who are rapidly "reopening the economy" in line with the Trump administration, including Gavin Newsom of California, Andrew Cuomo of New York, Gretchen Whitmer of Michigan, and more.

The pro-Democratic Party perspective, and the role of the Green Party more generally, was clearly expressed in an online Q&A session held on May 19 with Hawkins and Walker.

Hawkins explained that the role of the Green Party is not to "spoil" elections for the Democrats, but the exact opposite, to ensure that they win: "In my experience, I'm living in a congressional district where the only time a Democrat beat the Republicans since the Vietnam War…was when a Green was in the race. And of course, we were told we're splitting the vote. But what we did was change the dynamic. And the Democrat, instead of trying to talk like the Republican-light and get votes in the middle, had to deal with us and our positions, and they made them sound a lot better."

Hawkins expressed satisfaction that they were able to help the Democrats win, stating emphatically, "We improve elections, we don't spoil them!"

Taken at his word, Hawkins is saying that the Greens have helped elect numerous Democrats over the past four decades. During this period, the Democrats, no less than the Republicans, have presided over endless war and a massive transfer of wealth from the working class to the rich.

Responding to the question, "Are there any demands, policies your campaign could pressure Biden on?" Hawkins replied, "I think all the things that made Bernie Sanders popular—Medicare for All, Green New Deal, Economic Bill of Rights, student and medical debt relief—[Biden's] vulnerable, and we have leverage because Sanders got a lot of votes, and we're the only campaign real clear about we're for those things. And I think that gives us leverage on Biden."

In his typically muddled fashion, Hawkins added, "Of course, the thing you gotta watch out is, politicians make promises that they don't follow through. And so, even if he does move our way, we should remain insistent. He gotta earn those votes. If people believe him, okay they believe him. If they're skeptical, we're still here."

In other words, Hawkins' strategy is the same as Sanders—that Biden can be pushed to the left. This is, in fact, a political fraud. Biden personifies the Democratic Party as a party of Wall Street and the military. Sanders is now campaigning all out to get his supporters to back Biden, as he did with Clinton in 2016. He has gone so far as to threaten his delegates that their position will be revoked if they publicly criticize Biden.

The position of Hawkins and the Greens is not fundamentally different. Throughout his campaign, Hawkins has made clear he has no principled differences with Sanders or the politics of the Democratic Party as a whole. This was sharply expressed following Sanders's announcement that he was suspending his campaign, which led Hawkins to offer Sanders the Green Party candidacy, just as Jill Stein did in 2016.

As a trustworthy Democrat, Sanders snubbed the Greens, endorsed Biden, and branded as "irresponsible" anyone that didn't campaign for Biden, none of which has prompted any significant statement of criticism from Hawkins or the Green Party as a whole.

The real essence of the politics of the Green Party was summed up by Hawkins and Walker when they declared that their aim after the election is to create "a united front of independent non-sectarian left parties."

"Non-sectarian" as used by Hawkins and other organizations of the pseudo-left, means everyone except the Socialist Equality Party. By "sectarian" they mean any organization that rejects a political orientation to the Democratic Party and seeks to build a genuine socialist leadership in the working class.

In creating this "united front" against socialism, the Green Party hopes to serve as a halfway house for various pseudo-left organizations that had been promoting Sanders, including the Democratic Socialists of America (DSA), Socialist Alternative (SA), Socialist Party USA, Solidarity and other smaller parties. Each of these organizations operates in or around the Democratic Party, but some have been hesitant to openly support Biden, fearing that this will discredit them in the eyes of young people who are under the impression that they are socialist organizations.

A final word on the role of the Green Party internationally. Wherever the Greens have come to power, they have rapidly abandoned their so-called principles and collaborated with bourgeois parties to uphold the interests of the financial oligarchy.

This found its highest expression in Germany, where from 1998 to 2005 the Green Party joined the federal government for the first time in a "Red-Green" coalition government. While in power, the Greens oversaw the first German combat mission since World War II, the NATO war in Serbia, while helping force through the Hartz IV labor laws, the most sweeping attack on welfare programs in Germany in the post-war period. They have supported every foreign mission by the Bundeswehr since then, including the wars in Afghanistan, Iraq, Syria and Libya, while scapegoating refugees fleeing these wars.

The Austrian Greens this year entered into a coalition government with the right-wing conservative Austrian People's Party, and immediately adopted the policies of the far-right Freedom Party, including anti-immigrant measures. In New Zealand, Australia and other countries, the Greens have supported their respective imperialist governments in the drive to war. In the present situation, in which the ruling classes internationally are enforcing a homicidal policy of "reopening the economy" under unsafe conditions, the Greens in power in Austria and Germany have wholeheartedly endorsed this campaign.

Were Hawkins or any other Green Party politician to come to power in the US, their nationalist outlook would compel them to enforce the dictates of the American financial oligarchy, including through policies of war and austerity.

Like Sanders, moreover, Hawkins has sanctioned the neo-McCarthyism of the Democrats, supporting their anti-Russia campaign and their efforts to channel mass opposition to Trump behind the military and intelligence agencies. In an interview last year with YouTuber PRIMO NUTMEG, Hawkins stated, "The media is following this Russiagate thing, which I think is serious, and I think Trump ought to be impeached. I think it's obvious he sought collusion, he did collude, him and his son, his son-in-law. It's all over there, in that first volume of the Mueller report, it's all over there!"

In the same interview, Hawkins also endorsed the show trial of Julian Assange, who has been persecuted since 2010 for exposing the crimes of American imperialism. Responding to the question, "Do you think WikiLeaks was involved in this Russian plot?" Hawkins replied, "There's circumstantial evidence, like where are the WikiLeaks about Putin?" He added, "That remains to be seen if he was working with the Russians, or just biased with them. We'll see, I'm not sure."

In class terms, the Green Party is a party of the upper middle class. It is hostile to the working class and the development of a genuine socialist movement against capitalism. In its statements and commentary, it ignores the growth of working-class opposition while attempting to bolster the trade unions, which function as arms of corporate management and cheap labor police forces.

All of the great problems confronting the working class today—the COVID-19 pandemic, mass poverty, climate change and other ecological catastrophes, and the ever-present danger of a Third World War—are global in scope and can only be resolved through international socialist revolution. Any deviation from internationalism represents an opportunist sacrifice of the long-term interests of the working class.

The conditions wrought by the pandemic are radicalizing masses of workers and youth internationally, and the necessary task is to build a revolutionary socialist vanguard in the working class to lead the coming struggles to victory.

The only political movement in the world fighting for this perspective is the ICFI. In the 2020 elections in the US, the SEP is running Joseph Kishore for president and Norissa Santa Cruz for vice president, in a campaign whose aim is to educate the international working class on the principles of revolutionary socialism, popularize our program to combat the pandemic and overthrow capitalism, and fight to recruit the most advanced workers and youth to our party. We urge all those interested in genuine socialism to get involved with our campaign and contact us today.

> "Because the American political
> system makes it difficult for third
> parties to participate, Green Party
> candidates do not have opportunities
> to learn the trade of politics."

# The US Green Party Is Irrelevant

*Per Urlaub*

*In the following article, Per Urlaub discusses the political campaign of Jill Stein. Stein was the Green Party's nominee for US president in both the 2012 and 2016 elections. The author compares Stein's presidential campaign to Green Party successes in Europe from around the same era. He notes that political systems with proportional representation allow even small political parties to have a voice. That, along with a willingness to compromise, is what allowed Green Party candidates to gain power in Europe. In the author's view, the American Green Party will never compete with the Democratic and Republican Parties as long as the current system persists. Per Urlaub is an associate college professor at Middlebury College, Vermont, where he teaches in the linguistics program.*

"Why Is the US Green Party so Irrelevant?" by Per Urlaub, The Conversation, October 17, 2016. https://theconversation.com/why-is-the-us-green-party-so-irrelevant-66185. Licensed under CC-BY-ND-4.0 International.

As you read, consider the following questions:

1. How does proportional representation allow small political parties to have a voice?
2. Why is compromise important in politics, according to the author?
3. Why are third parties unable to compete with the Democratic and Republican Parties, according to the author?

Many Americans value environmental protection and want to see more of it. But Jill Stein, the Green Party presidential candidate, is drawing only 1 to 3 percent in recent polls, even in an election where many voters dislike the major candidates and are looking for alternatives.

Stein certainly has worked to differentiate herself from the two major party candidates. In July she asserted that electing Democratic nominee Hillary Clinton—probably the choice of most pro-environment voters—would "fan the flames of … right-wing extremism," and be as bad as electing Donald Trump.

While Stein makes anti-establishment statements like this, her German counterparts have been advancing a green agenda in local, regional and national government for the past 30 years. Most recently, Winfried Kretschmann was reelected this year as head of government in Baden-Württemberg, one of Europe's technologically and industrially most advanced regions.

I grew up in Germany and have taught about Germany and Europe in the United States for the past 15 years, so I have seen Green Party politicians at work in both countries. In my view, there are two reasons why the US Green Party remains so marginal. Structurally, the American electoral system is heavily weighted against small political parties. But US Greens also harm themselves by taking extreme positions and failing to understand that governing requires compromise—a lesson their German counterparts learned several decades ago.

## One Movement, Two Electoral Systems

Both European and North American Green Parties evolved from activist movements in the 1960s that focused on causes including environmentalism, disarmament, nuclear power, nonviolence, reproductive rights and gender equality. West German Greens formed a national political party in 1980 and gained support in local, state and federal competitions. Joschka Fischer, one of the first Greens elected to Germany's Bundestag (parliament), served as the nation's foreign minister and vice chancellor from 1998-2005.

The German Green Party's rise owed much to the country's electoral system. As in many continental European democracies, political parties win seats in German elections based on the percentage of voters that support them. For example, a party winning a third of the popular vote will hold roughly a third of the seats in the parliament after the election. Proportional representation makes it possible for small parties to gain a toehold and build a presence in government over time.

In contrast, US elections award seats on a winner-takes-all basis. The candidate with the most votes wins, while votes cast for candidates representing other parties are ignored. As a result, American voters choose their leaders within a de facto two-party system in which other parties often have trouble even getting their candidates' names onto ballots.

US Greens have won only a handful of state-level races, and have never won a congressional seat. Their greatest success came in 2000, when Ralph Nader and Winona LaDuke won 2.7 percent of the popular vote in the presidential election. Many observers argued that Nader's only real impact was to throw the election to conservative Republican George W. Bush, but Nader and many of his supporters strongly disagreed, and the question of whether challengers can act as more than spoilers in US elections remains controversial today.

## Purity or Compromise?

As green politicians have helped to shape political priorities in Berlin, Brussels and other European capitals and regions, many observers have debated whether these former activists are selling out by participating in the political process—and whether joining that process helps or hurts the green movement.

During the 1980s and early 1990s, Green Party conventions in Germany were dominated by fierce infighting between moderate "Realos" (realists) and radical "Fundis" (fundamentalists). The Realos, who prioritized electability over ideology, eventually prevailed.

In order to graduate from an opposition party to a ruling party that controlled cabinet posts, German Greens had to develop a capacity for compromise. To gain power, they had to form coalitions with center-left Social Democrats. But coalitions require consensus—especially in parliaments with proportional representation.

Interacting with centrist politicians, unionists, church representatives and the media taught Realos to act less like activists and more like politicians. In 1998 the Green Party formed a so-called red-green coalition with the Social Democratic Party (SPD), a party that has traditionally championed the working class, and won a large majority in the Bundestag.

Working through this alliance, former activists initiated reform of an antiquated immigration and citizenship law and worked toward recognition of same-sex unions. They implemented an environmentally driven tax code and brokered a deal with the nuclear energy industry to cancel projects for new plants and phase out nuclear power by 2022.

Many Green Party supporters thought Realos were too eager to compromise. Some even physically attacked their party leaders when the coalition government supported use of military force in a NATO-led campaign against Serbia in 1999. Many critics viewed this decision as the remilitarization of German foreign policy under the leadership of Joschka Fischer of the Green Party, then serving as Foreign Minister.

However, these compromises did not erode broad public support for the Greens. On the contrary, in 2002 the red-green coalition was reelected and the Green Party received more votes than it had in 1998. When the coalition government broke down in 2005, it was due to Chancellor Gerhard Schröder's lack of leadership within his own SPD.

Although the Green Party has not regained control of Germany's federal government since 2005, its positions have become part of the nation's mainstream political culture. Notably, after the 2011 nuclear plant meltdown in Fukushima, Japan, a center-right German government decided to accelerate the phaseout of nuclear power in response to rising public concern. To reach this goal, Angela Merkel's centrist government has implemented an ambitious policy bundle known as the Energiewende that seeks to transition Germany to a nonnuclear, low-carbon energy future.

Massive governmental support for alternative energy sources has encouraged Germans, especially in rural areas, to invest in solar power, wind turbines and biomass plants. These green policies did not harm, and may have buoyed, Merkel's status as one of the most popular German chancellors prior to this year's controversies over immigration. Germany reformed its renewable energy law this year in response to new European Union rules governing electricity markets, and will shift from subsidies to market-based mechanisms, but the Energiewende remains highly popular.

## No Third Lane

There is no easy way for the US Green Party to emulate its German counterparts. Because the American political system makes it difficult for third parties to participate, Green Party candidates do not have opportunities to learn the trade of politics. They have remained activists who are true to their base instead of developing policy positions that would appeal to a broader audience. By doing so, they weaken their chances of winning major races even in liberal strongholds.

As a result, green ideas enter American political debates only when Democrats and Republicans take up these issues. It is telling that major US environmental groups started endorsing Clinton even before she had clinched the Democratic presidential nomination over Bernie Sanders, who took more aggressive positions on some environmental and energy issues during their primary contest. And although Sanders identifies as an environmentalist, he sought the Democratic Party nomination instead of running as the Green Party candidate.

This suggests that running on a third-party ticket in the United States is still not a winning route to shaping a message aimed at a broad electorate. Instead, climate change, dwindling energy resources and growing human and economic costs from natural disasters will do more to promote ecological consciousness and political change in mainstream America than the radical rhetoric of the US Green Party.

*"In practice, they orient politically to the Democratic Party, promoting the fatal illusion that this instrument of American imperialism, controlled top to bottom by Wall Street, can be pressured from below to adopt progressive policies and transform itself into a party of the common people."*

# Don't Be Fooled by the Green Party

*Tom Hall*

*In the following viewpoint, Tom Hall argues that the Green Party promotes itself as a party to push the Democrats further left and also as a solution to the bipartisan gridlock of current US politics. However, he maintains that in reality it is just as dependent on Wall Street and capitalism as other political parties in the United States. The author addresses the Green Party platform from a socialist perspective, noting that the Green platform caters to the privilege of the upper middle class and fails to represent workers. Tom Hall is a writer for the World Socialist Web Site.*

"The Pro-Capitalist Program of the US Green Party," by Tom Hall, World Socialist Web Site, July 23, 2016. Reprinted by permission.

As you read, consider the following questions:

1. Why does the author refer to the Green Party platform as an "unprincipled, eclectic combination of demands"?
2. According to the viewpoint, how does the Green Party promote capitalism?
3. How does the US Green Party differ from the Green Party in other countries, according to the author?

The 2016 US presidential campaign has revealed an extraordinary crisis of legitimacy of American capitalist politics. In spite of a primary campaign whose dominant features were growing social opposition and deep alienation among voters from both the Democratic and Republicans parties, the American public faces the prospect in November of choosing between the two most hated presidential candidates in modern American history, with Hillary Clinton, the multimillionaire stooge of Wall Street and the military/intelligence establishment on the one hand, and Donald Trump, the fascistic billionaire on the other.

The election has unfolded against the background of growing social opposition in the working class in the United States and internationally. In the primary election campaign, this found its most significant expression, and from the standpoint of the ruling elite, the most worrying, in the broad support for the campaign for the Democratic nomination of the self-described "socialist" Bernie Sanders. This has revealed that in a country whose political life has long been dominated by anticommunism, millions of people hold anti-capitalist views.

Sanders, however, is not a socialist, but a longstanding congressional ally of the Democratic Party. From the outset, his aim in running was to channel social and political opposition back within the harmless channels of the Democratic Party, long the graveyard of social movements in the United States, by means of left-sounding slogans such as his call for a "political revolution" against the "billionaire class."

Nevertheless, many of his supporters reacted with shock and anger to his endorsement earlier this month of Hillary Clinton, the favored candidate of most of corporate America.

The remaining months before the November election promise to be explosive. Under these conditions, the Green Party is positioning itself as the next line of defense against the emergence of an independent political and socialist movement of the working class. The Green Party and its presumptive presidential candidate Jill Stein have been hard at work in recent weeks appealing to disillusioned Sanders supporters and portraying themselves as a genuinely independent "left" political alternative.

The emptiness of this claim of political independence has already been graphically demonstrated in the current election campaign. Both before and after Sanders announced his withdrawal from the Democratic primary race and endorsement of Clinton, Jill Stein publicly offered to withdraw her candidacy if Sanders agreed to become the presidential candidate of the US Green Party. Sanders summarily rejected the offer.

Workers and youth must learn to analyze and assess all political organizations not by their "left" presentation of themselves or their nominal organizational independence from the Democratic Party, but by their "history, program, perspective, and class basis and orientation," as the Socialist Equality Party explains in its Statement of Principles.

An examination of the most recent platform of the Green Party, ratified in July of 2014, demonstrates the reactionary character of the party's politics. The Green Party is a bourgeois party, representing the interests of privileged strata of the upper-middle class. It is steeped in nationalism, defends capitalist property relations and opposes the political independence of the working class.

## A Middle-Class Program

The platform is divided into four chapters, but begins with a number of introductory sections. On the first page of the platform, titled "About the Green Party," it states: "The Green Party of the United States is a federation of state Green Parties. Committed to environmentalism, non-violence, social justice and grassroots organizing, Greens are renewing democracy without the support of corporate donors."

It continues: "Greens provide real solutions for real problems. Whether the issue is universal health care, corporate globalization, alternative energy, election reform or decent, living wages for workers, Greens have the courage and independence necessary to take on the powerful corporate interests."

This introduction already demonstrates the middle-class character of the Greens. Despite their denunciation of "corporate-dominated politics," they do not mention capitalism, socialism or the working class in describing their orientation. Instead, they invoke nebulous slogans without any specific class content, such as "renewing democracy" and providing "real solutions for real problems."

The platform continues with the party's "Call to Action" statement. This explicitly defines the role of the Green Party as serving as an external (from an organizational standpoint) pressure group on the two major parties and the capitalist two-party system. It states: "The United States is locked in a vicious circle, in which it has become increasingly clear that the 'bipartisan' political duopoly will drift further rightward at an increasing pace without a true opposition party as a counterweight, as both corporate parties seek to better serve their 1 percent masters."

This makes clear that the Greens' political perspective is to gain access to the political establishment in order to pressure it to the left. They themselves define their role as serving as a satellite of the capitalist establishment, rendering their claim to political independence utterly empty and dishonest. In practice, they orient politically to the Democratic Party, promoting the fatal illusion that this instrument of American imperialism, controlled top to bottom by Wall Street, can be pressured from below to adopt progressive policies and transform itself into a party of the common people.

The same section concludes with a veiled attack on Marxism and profession of political eclecticism and pragmatism. It states: "Now is the time to discard failed ideologies and political structures [having just called for reforming the existing political structure], and join together with the flourishing global grassroots Green movement to tackle real problems with real solutions." This is a recipe for the most craven political opportunism, which is borne out in the rest of the document.

More will be said about the politics of the "flourishing global grassroots Green movement." For now, it is sufficient to point out that this includes Green parties in Germany, Australia and other countries that have either joined or supported capitalist governments that brutally attacked the working class and waged war in the Balkans, Afghanistan, the Middle East and elsewhere.

Next comes the "Preamble." This section includes an explicit defense of the capitalist market, calling for a "regulated market economy." Far from a left-wing or even revolutionary party, the Greens advocate not a fundamental restructuring of society, but at most a return to the sort of nationally regulated equilibrium that predominated in the years after World War II.

This same section invokes a number of political tropes that are standard fare in right-wing capitalist politics. It strikes an economic nationalist posture by focusing its criticism on economic policy on the export of jobs to other countries, without relating this to the capitalist system itself: "Jobs are being permanently relocated outside the country."

It complains about government deficits, suggesting a justification for austerity: "Every single level of government—local, county, state and federal—is operating in the red, running up crushing amounts of debt."

It speaks of social justice and equal opportunity, "emphasizing personal and social responsibility, accountability and an informing ethic of Nonviolence." In other words, the poor and downtrodden bear individual responsibility for their plight and had better "shape up."

By means of honeyed and banal phrases, it rejects the class struggle and preaches class collaboration, calling for "a democratic structure and process that empowers and reaches across lines of division to bring together our combined strengths as a people."

Under the heading "Ten Key Values," the platform relegates social class to the status of a subsidiary aspect of identity politics, declaring: "We must consciously confront in ourselves, our organizations, and society at large, barriers such as racism and class oppression, sexism and homophobia, ageism and disability, which act to deny fair treatment and equal justice under the law." "Key Values" number 7 is devoted entirely to "Feminism and Gender Equality."

In the name of "ecological wisdom," this section of the platform broaches the reactionary Malthusian conceptions that form an essential component of Green Party politics, declaring that "we must live within the ecological and resource limits of our communities and our planet." Key Value number 10 ("Future Focus and Sustainability") spells out more explicitly the backward, anti-growth bias of the Greens, calling for a "sustainable economics that does not depend on continual expansion for survival."

Under "non-violence," the platform qualifies its ostensible pacifism so as to make the Green Party acceptable to the political establishment, writing: "We will work to demilitarize, and eliminate weapons of mass destruction, without being naïve about the intentions of other governments. We recognize the need for self-defense and the defense of others who are in helpless situations." This translates in practice into support for the diplomatic and military intrigues of American imperialism, including support for imperialist wars (Libya, Syria, Iraq) fought under the pretext of "human rights."

As a whole, the Green Party platform is an unprincipled, eclectic combination of demands, extending across 71 pages, which are guided by no unifying political perspective or analysis and which often run at cross-purposes with one another. The one constant throughout is a superficial approach to every question, a hallmark of all types of middle-class politics, which consistently slurs over or ignores the fundamental class issues and rejects an approach to politics based on an historical analysis.

The basic orientation of the document as a whole is a narrow, parochial nationalism. Almost all of the Green Party's political demands proceed entirely from the standpoint of reforms to be carried out within the United States.

In the whole of the document, the term "socialism" appears only once, in a pejorative connection. There is no mention of the crisis of American and world capitalism.

The question of social inequality is decidedly downplayed. To they extent that the Greens offer any solution to the problems of poverty and joblessness, it is to "move beyond the narrow 'job ethic' to new definitions of 'work,' 'jobs' and 'income' that reflect the changing economy." In other words, to redefine the problems out of existence.

The Green Party accepts and defends capitalist property relations. It rejects the nationalization of the banks and major corporations under the democratic control of working people in favor of "[reducing] the size and concentrated power of corporations without discouraging superior efficiency or technological innovation." Instead of workers' control of production, the Greens call for "employee ownership and workplace democracy," which, later on in the document, resolves itself into explicit support for the corporatist collaboration of the trade union bureaucracy with capitalist management.

## Silence on Imperialist War

There is no mention in the "Call to Action," the "Preamble" or the "Ten Key Values" of the danger of war or the criminal role of American imperialism. In the remaining 66 pages of the platform, across four chapters titled "Democracy," "Social Justice," "Ecological Sustainability," and "Economic Justice and Sustainability," there is not a single heading that refers to war or imperialism. This is the case in a document published in the 13th year of the "war on terror," in the midst of the war in Afghanistan and the US war for regime-change in Syria, with the US-backed war in Gaza underway, and the death and destruction wreaked in Iraq and Libya continuing to claim lives and drive masses from their homes.

When this platform was published, moreover, the United States was already in the third year of its anti-Chinese "pivot to Asia" and was in the process of escalating its offensive against Russia begun with the US-backed putsch that overthrew a pro-Russian government in Ukraine. Civil war was raging in eastern Ukraine, with the US backing troops of the right-wing nationalist regime in Kiev and neo-fascist militias sent to put down the separatist rebellion of Russian-speaking provinces.

Germany had announced its plans to rearm and take on an aggressive posture in Europe and beyond, and Japan had declared its intention of repudiating pacifist provisions of its constitution in order to once again become a major military power.

The silence of the Greens under these conditions could mean only one thing: subordination to US imperialism and its drive toward a third world war.

## The International Record

The class character of the Greens as a political tendency is demonstrated by the record of Green parties internationally, many of which have entered government or played crucial roles in their respective countries' political systems. The record of betrayals and political reaction is an indication of what can be expected if the US Greens win greater political influence.

The US Green Party's platform makes only passing reference to this record, sandwiched in between the cover page and the table of contents, when it states that it is "partners with the European Federation of Green Parties and the Federation of Green Parties of the Americas."

The German Greens, the largest and most important member of the European Federation of Green Parties, and whose initial electoral successes in the early 1980s were the impetus for the formation of the US Green movement, became the first Green Party to enter a national government in 1998, the so-called "red-green coalition" with the German Social Democratic Party.

The Greens immediately dropped their longstanding programmatic commitment to pacifism and became full-throated supporters of the NATO air war in Serbia, the German military's first foreign deployment since the end of World War II. As part of the same coalition government, they helped force through the Hartz IV labor laws, the most sweeping attack on welfare programs in Germany since the end of the war.

Since then, they have supported sending German troops to Afghanistan, backed the German- and US-sponsored coup in Ukraine, and endorsed German involvement in the wars in Libya, Iraq and Syria. They are among the most bellicose parties in parliament in their support for Germany's aggressive moves against Russia. They have played a leading role in the scapegoating of refugees fleeing the US-led and German-supported proxy wars in the Middle East.

They have also assumed responsibility for attacks on the working class at the state level. In April, the German Greens entered into a coalition government in the state of Baden-Württemberg with the Christian Democratic Union, Germany's principal conservative party and the party of the current chancellor, Angela Merkel.

The Green Party in Australia, affiliated with the US Greens through the Global Greens Network, played a critical role in propping up the hated minority Labor government of Julia Gillard from 2010 to 2013 through the cross-bench support of their party's sole member of parliament. The Gillard government was one of the most right-wing in the country's history. It greatly expanded Australia's involvement in US-led military operations and lined up fully behind Washington's war preparations against China carried out in the name of the "pivot to Asia." It slashed funding for health care, education and welfare programs and continued the brutal anti-refugee policies of previous administrations.

The US Greens might contend that they are not responsible for the activities of their international affiliates—an inherently false and unprincipled position. In any case, the reactionary record of Green Parties internationally is not the result of bad choices by individual leaders or national parties, but rather the inevitable consequence of the pro-capitalist and nationalist political orientation and perspective at the heart of the entire international Green movement.

# Periodical and Internet Sources Bibliography

*The following articles have been selected to supplement the diverse views presented in this chapter.*

Fadel Allassan, "Over 170 Environmental Leaders Urge Supporters Not to Vote for Green Party," Axios, September 14, 2020. https://www.axios.com/environmental-leaders-green-party-biden-trump-de76c6cd-38df-47e3-90c1-00f92774f3f1.html

Linda Averill, "The Green Party: Offering a Real Challenge to Business as Usual, or Just Capitalism Lite?" Freedom Socialist Party, December 2006. https://socialism.com/fs-article/the-green-party-offering-a-real-challenge-to-business-as-usual-or-just-capitalism-lite/

Penelope Carroll, Sally Casswell, John Huakau, Paul Perry, and Philippa Howden Chapman, "Environmental Attitudes, Beliefs About Social Justice and Intention to Vote Green: Lessons for the New Zealand Green Party?" *Environmental Politics*, Volume 18, February 27, 2009. https://www.tandfonline.com/doi/abs/10.1080/09644010802682635?journalCode=fenp20

Tim Cotton, "Social Justice and Equal Opportunity Are Green Party Values," *Culpeper Star-Exponent*, April 13, 2017. https://starexponent.com/opinion/column-social-justice-and-equal-opportunity-are-green-party-values/article_90f3b5e2-a841-55f1-a019-4cf3a86a7ddc.html

Nathaniel Flakin, "Can the Green Party Be a Vehicle for Socialists? A European Perspective," Left Voice, September 26, 2020. https://www.leftvoice.org/can-the-green-party-be-a-vehicle-for-socialists-a-european-perspective/

Zack P. Grant, "When Are Green Parties Successful," EUROPP, December 5, 2018. https://blogs.lse.ac.uk/europpblog/2018/12/05/when-are-green-parties-successful/

Green Party US, "Social Justice and Equality." https://www.gp.org/social_justice_and_equality

Tom Hall, "The Pro-Capitalist Program of the US Green Party," World Socialist Web Site, July 23, 2016. https://www.wsws.org/en/articles/2016/07/23/gree-j23.html

Emma Graham Harrison, "A Quiet Revolution Sweeps Europe as Greens Become a Political Force, *The Guardian*, June 2, 2019. https://www.theguardian.com/politics/2019/jun/02/european -parliament-election-green-parties-success

Left Unity, "Just How Left Wing Is the Green Party?" http://leftunity .org/just-how-left-wing-is-the-green-party/

Ferdinand Müller-Rommel, "The Greens in Western Europe: Similar but Different," *International Political Science Review*, Vol. 6, No. 4, Sage Publications, Ltd. https://www.jstor.org/stable/1601056

Ash Murphy, "Will Politicians Take Action and Try to Save the Planet from Climate Change?" The Conversation, September 16, 2019. https://theconversation.com/will-politicians-take-action-and-try -to-save-the-planet-from-climate-change-122754

John Rensenbrink, "Challenge and Response," Green Party US, February 2003. https://www.gp.org/challenge_and_response

**OPPOSING
VIEWPOINTS®
SERIES**

# CHAPTER 3

# Do Americans
# Need or Want the
# Green Party?

# Chapter Preface

Many Americans believe they should have more than two choices when it comes to politics. Polls show that up to 60 percent of Americans want an alternative party. With only two parties, politicians with widely different views are forced into the same box. In 2020, Alexandria Ocasio-Cortez noted, "In any other country, Joe Biden and I would not be in the same party." Yet because the US does not have a major party for progressives, anyone to the left tends to vote Democrat.

In US politics, anyone who wants a chance to win a major election needs to ally with a major party. Third-party candidates have won some local elections and a few state elections, but even those are rare. This leads many people to claim voting for third-party candidates is a waste because a third-party candidate has virtually no chance of winning a major election.

Some people even blame third-party candidates for another party's loss. In the 2016 election, the Green Party's candidate for president, Jill Stein, took votes away from Hillary Clinton. Although that does not explain the Democratic candidate's loss, many people blamed the Green Party. They were even less likely to vote Green in 2020. Meanwhile, the Republican Party supported getting Green Party candidates onto the 2020 ballot. The Republicans hoped to benefit by giving liberals choices that would divide their vote.

When two parties hold almost all of the power, they make the rules. The Democrats and Republicans have been passing laws to make it ever more difficult for a third party to get on election ballots. Third-party candidates are kept out of the major political debates. Major media outlets rarely bother to cover third-party activities, since it's clear they won't win.

Furthermore, most corporate money and other large donations go to the major parties. The Republicans and Democrats together spent nearly $14 billion on the 2020 presidential election. Money buys advertising space, supports outreach, and pays for candidates to travel and speak to the public. In return, the politicians who received that money may feel like they owe favors to the billionaires or corporations who funded their campaign.

When they can't reach the public through ads or media coverage, third-party candidates struggle to educate the public on how they are different. Donors want to give their money where it will do the most good. Voters want to vote for a candidate who has a chance of winning. The system keeps third-party candidates far, far behind.

Does this mean the Green Party has no place in America? Not necessarily. Even if the party gets few votes, it may help shift the conversation. Sometimes a third party such as the Green Party can bring to light an issue until it grows in the public's concern, such as the environment and global climate change. Then one or both of the major parties starts addressing the issue. They may borrow ideas from a third party, claiming those ideas as their own. The Green Party has proposed policies that have been adopted by the Democratic Party. For some, that alone is enough for the Green Party to justify its existence. For others, the future lies in developing a system that allows additional parties to have more of a voice in government.

The following chapter shares viewpoints on whether the Green Party is beneficial or even necessary to the United States.

> *"Amid the government shutdown, 60% of Americans say the Democratic and Republican parties do such a poor job of representing the American people that a third major party is needed."*

# America Is Ready for a Third Party

*Nick Wright*

*In the following viewpoint, Nick Wright addresses a poll that concluded that many Americans are at least interested in another major political party. At that time, the Green Party claimed it could be the new third party. The author quotes several Green Party leaders who shared why they thought the party's time had come. These leaders claimed Americans weren't getting what they wanted and needed from the Republican and Democratic Parties. In their view, the United States needs a party that represents working people. To do this, the party must refuse corporate contributions. Nick Wright is an editor and writer with 21centurymanifesto, which reports on working-class political issues in Britain.*

"Green Party: '60% of Americans Want an Alternative Party? Let's Talk,'" by Nick Wright, 21 Manifesto, November 7, 2013. Reprinted by permission.

As you read, consider the following questions:

1. How would the Green Party change health care in the US?
2. Why might women be especially interested in the Green Party, according to the viewpoint?
3. What is the problem with politicians taking corporate money, according to the Green Party?

G reen Party candidates and leaders said that a recent Gallup poll shows that the recent shutdown left millions of Americans feeling betrayed by both Democrats and Republicans in Washington and open to a major new political party.

According to the poll, "Amid the government shutdown, 60% of Americans say the Democratic and Republican parties do such a poor job of representing the American people that a third major party is needed." ("In US, Perceived Need for Third Party Reaches New High" Oct. 11.)

Greens called the shutdown, which might reoccur soon as Congress and the White House continue budget negotiations, an opportunity for Americans to discuss the future of US democracy and ending domination by two parties.

Joe DeMare, Green candidate for Bowling Green City Council in Ohio: "Americans are realizing that the shutdown is a symptom of two-party politics. The shutdown revealed Republicans as the party of irresponsible extremists, but Democrats have also moved far to the right. The solution to shutdowns, sequestration, and the politics of war and Wall Street isn't compromise or the phony center between the Ds and the Rs. The solution is multiparty democracy and the end of two-party rule. The shutdown proved that America needs a party that refuses corporate contributions and that represents working people—including federal and state employees. That's why we call the Green Party an imperative for the 21st century."

Alfred Molison, Texas Green and a federal employee: "Social Security and Medicare are in danger from both parties. Much of the Obama Administration's agenda and accomplishments, including the Affordable Care Act and plans to slash Social Security, would have been recognized as Republican ten years ago. The individual mandate was introduced by the Heritage Foundations and promoted by Republicans until Democrats made it the basis of the ACA. The bipartisan debate over the ACA is between two factions that want to keep our health care under the control of for-profit insurance company gatekeepers. The Green Party continues to demand Medicare For All—single-payer national health care, in which patients and physicians, not corporate bureaucrats, make decisions about medical care."

Lynne Serpe, Green candidate for New York City Council, District 22 in Queens: "The movement for an alternative party will grow as more Americans vote independently. But we also need election reforms, like Instant Runoff Voting, Proportional Representation, caps on political contributions, public funding for campaigns and repeal of election laws in many states that privilege Democratic and Republican politicians and obstruct other candidates and parties. Greens have advocated these changes since the party was founded and we're helping to lead the struggle to make the US a real democracy."

Marian Douglas-Ungaro, activist for statehood and equal rights in the District of Columbia and member of the DC Statehood Green Party: "Women are among those hardest hit by sequestration, austerity measures, and the recent shutdown. Women stand the most to lose from deals between the White House and Congress to shred the safety net and scale back earned benefits. Greens have different priorities: Cheri Honkala, the Green Party's 2012 vice-presidential nominee, helped host a meeting in Philadelphia this past weekend of the World Court of Women that focused on poverty. Women of all backgrounds deserve a political party that we can build from the bottom up. Democrats and Republicans measure the health of the US economy according to Dow Jones, the GDP, and corporate profit reports. Greens judge the economy according to how many people are lifted out of poverty."

Laura Wells, Green candidate for California Controller in the 2014 election: "Richmond, California is the best example of government for the people, not corporations. It is the largest city in the US with a Green Party mayor. Gayle McLaughlin is a champion of solutions for people, and stands up to the biggest corporation in the state, Chevron. Now she's taking on Wall Street banks, intending to use eminent domain if necessary to keep people in their homes. Why did she move on that idea and other mayors did not? Because she's a Green and takes no corporate money. My favorite election ever was in Richmond in 2010 when Chevron put $1 million into three races and lost, lost, and lost. The candidates who took no corporate money won. And the people won."

> "Greens don't spoil elections. We
> improve them. We advance solutions
> that otherwise won't get raised."

# Stop Blaming the Green Party for Democrats' Failures

*Howie Hawkins*

*In the following viewpoint, Howie Hawkins challenges the idea that the Green Party hurts the Democrats. He claims that the Electoral College was responsible for Democratic presidential losses in 2000 and 2016. The Electoral College system assigns each state a certain number of votes, cast by representatives, instead of counting the popular vote nationwide. Hawkins insists that the Green Party is needed to address many of the problems the country and world face. In addition, it needs to run a presidential candidate in order to get local candidates on the ballots. Hawkins was the 2020 Green Party candidate for president in the US.*

As you read, consider the following questions:

1. How did the Electoral College cause Democratic candidates to lose the presidential elections?
2. Why is the Green Party made up of frustrated Democrats?
3. What would the Green Party use to replace the Electoral College?

Although it is a constant refrain from Democratic leaders and commentators, the Green Party is not why the Democrats lost to Bush and Trump.

In trying to excuse her loss to Trump, Hillary Clinton recently made the baseless smears that Jill Stein, the Greens' 2016 presidential candidate, is a "Russian asset," and that Russians and Republicans are "grooming" a third party challenger for 2020.

Cornell professor Glen C. Altschuler opined in *The Hill* last week that since the Green Party was the "spoiler" of the 2000 and 2016 presidential elections, "The 'Green' New Deal that Tom Perez needs to make" is to persuade the Green ticket to endorse the Democratic ticket in the swing states in 2020.

Altschuler is not facing reality. The Green Party is not going back to the "safe states strategy" that a faction of it attempted in 2004. It couldn't even be carried out. It alienated Greens in swing states who were working so hard to overcome onerous petitioning requirements to get the party on the ballot. Keeping the party on the ballot for the next election cycle for their local candidates depended on the Green presidential vote in many states. It became clear that safe states was dispiriting and demoralizing because the party didn't take itself seriously enough to justify its existence independent of the Democrats. Few people, even in the safe states, wanted to waste their vote for a Green ticket that was more concerned with electing the Democratic ticket than advancing its own demands, which in 2004 started with ending the war in Iraq that both Bush and Kerry wanted to escalate with a "surge" of more troops.

The assertion that the Green Party spoiled the 2000 and 2016 elections is a shallow explanation for the Democrats' losses.

It wasn't Ralph Nader who elected Bush in 2000. It was the Supreme Court. It stopped the Florida recount. A consortium of major news organizations later did a thorough recount. Gore won their statewide recounts.

It wasn't Jill Stein who elected Trump in 2016. It was many factors, including black voter suppression, Comey publicly reopening of the Clinton email case a week before the election, $6 billion of free publicity for Trump from the commercial media, and a Clinton campaign that failed to get enough of its Democratic base out.

In both cases, it was the Electoral College that gave the presidency to the loser of the popular vote.

To hold all other factors constant and focus on the Green Party as the deciding factor is a hypothetical that is a logical fallacy because it assumes away a factual reality: the Green Party is here to stay.

## THE GREEN THREAT TO DEMOCRATS

If the Democrats aren't liberal enough for some voters in North Carolina, there is now another choice. With Republican support, the "Electoral Freedom Act" reduced the number of signatures required for third parties to get on the ballot.

The Green Party is the only party that met the requirements and was welcomed by the Republican Party to North Carolina. Democrats were not as happy.

If you haven't figured it out, we'll say it because it's pretty obvious once you understand the background. Republicans have struggled with competition from the Libertarian Party for years. Libertarians are to Republicans as the Green Party is to Democrats. If Republicans aren't conservative enough, there is the Libertarian Party. Libertarians do join the Republican Party in many instances. But their third party candidates tend to siphon conservative votes.

Some of the extreme right-wing rants that make even Republicans cringe come from Libertarians. To be fair, there is also a good argument that some Democrat candidates attract Libertarian voters as Libertarians do share some views with the left, such as the position that abortion is an individual choice. But overall, conventional wisdom is third-party Libertarian candidates hurt Republicans more.

Now the Democratic Party gets a kindred spirit. Many Democrats will feel comfortable in the Green Party. The North Carolina Republican Party published a press release congratulating the Greens. The state Democratic Party didn't make a similar do so and for good reason.

If a Green Party candidate secures just 2 percent of the vote that would have otherwise gone to Democrats, then Republicans win.

"Greens Pose Threat to Democrats," *The Robesonian*, April 10, 2018.

The Green Party exists because it is needed. Most Greens are furious and former Democrats angry at a party that joins with Republicans to support pay-go domestic austerity and a bloated military budget and endless wars. Trump may call climate change a hoax. But the Democrats act as if it is a hoax.

A Green New Deal from Tom Perez? Is Altschuler serious? It was Perez who got the Democratic National Committee to recommit to donations from the fossil fuel industry and to Obama's "all-of-the-above" energy policy, which is a euphemism for fracking the hell out of the country for oil and gas. Obama continues to boast that his policy made the US the world's largest oil and gas producer.

The Green Party's signature issue for the last decade, the Green New Deal, would put the country on a World War II scale emergency footing to transform the economy to zero greenhouse gas emissions and 100% clean energy by 2030. No Democrat is campaigning for that program on that science-based timeline for averting mass climate carnage.

Inequality has been growing for 45 years under both Democratic and Republican administrations. Inequality kills. The life expectancy gap between America's richest and poorest counties is now over 20 years. The exasperated former Democrats in the Green Party want to eliminate poverty and radically reduce inequality by finally enacting the Economic Bill of Rights that FDR proposed in his last two State of the Union addresses in 1944 and 1945. Those rights should include a job guarantee, a guaranteed income above poverty, affordable housing, improved Medicare for all, lifelong public education from pre-K through college, and a secure retirement.

A new nuclear arms race has taken off while arms control treaties have been abandoned. None of the major party candidates "have a plan for that." How about a no-first-use pledge, unilateral disarmament to a minimum credible deterrent, and, on the basis of those tension-reducing initiatives, aggressively pursuing negotiations among the nuclear powers for complete nuclear disarmament? The US is obligated to negotiate nuclear disarmament under the 1970 Nuclear Non-Proliferation Treaty. The Treaty for the Prohibition of Nuclear Weapons, the text of which was approved by 122 non-nuclear nations in July 2017, demands it. The International Campaign to Abolish Nuclear Weapons received the Nobel Peace Prize for that achievement. Almost no one in America even knows that. The world is worried. Americans are kept ignorant. The major party candidates aren't talking about it.

Greens want to get Trump out as much as anybody. Our advice to Democrats is to stop worrying about the Green Party and focus on getting your own base out. Our position is that we are running our own candidates because neither corporate-indentured party will support real solutions to the life-or-death issues of climate change, growing inequality, and nuclear weapons.

The last two Republican presidents lost the popular vote when they were first elected. Instead of telling the Green Party to go away, or back the Democratic ticket, Democrats should join Greens in fighting to abolish the Electoral College and elect the president through a National Popular Vote using Ranked Choice Voting. That would end the vote-splitting spoiler problem.

The Greens must be in the presidential race to raise these demands. The Greens put solutions into public debate that the major parties refuse to support. That has been the historic role of third parties in the US since the Liberty Party put abolition on the political agenda. The Greenback Labor, People's, and Socialist parties first advanced social and economic reforms that later came to be adopted. That is a role Greens will continue to play.

But Greens have more ambitious goals. We want to build a major party that can defeat the two-capitalist-party system of corporate rule. We want to ally with other progressive and socialist parties for a united electoral front of the independent left. Our strategy is to build the party from the bottom up by electing thousands to municipal and county offices, state legislatures, and soon the House as we go into the 2020s. When the independent left has a caucus in Congress, then its presidential ticket will be competitive.

So why are we running a presidential ticket in 2020 if our strategy is to build the party from the bottom up? Because Greens need ballot lines to run local candidates. Securing ballot lines for the next election cycle is affected by the petition signatures and/or votes for our presidential ticket in 40 of the states.

Greens don't spoil elections. We improve them. We advance solutions that otherwise won't get raised. We are running out of time on the climate crisis, inequality, and nuclear weapons. Greens will be damned if we wait for the Democrats. Real solutions can't wait.

> *"Third-party candidates deserve a chance to pull votes from the Democratic or Republican Party, and the American people should have a chance to hear what they have to say."*

# Give the Green Party a Chance

*Micaela Warren*

*In the following viewpoint, Micaela Warren looks at the 2020 election and the dissatisfaction many people had with the two major parties. The author argues that the Green Party should have been allowed to join the major political debates. She suggests that many Americans agree with Green Party ideals, and therefore the party should be given a voice. Micaela Warren wrote this for the* Daily Orange, *Syracuse University's independent student newspaper.*

As you read, consider the following questions:

1. How were Green Party candidates "unrightfully silenced" during the 2020 election, according to the author?
2. How would limiting campaign spending help politicians who don't take money from big donors?
3. How does the Green Party separate itself from the Democratic Party, according to the viewpoint?

"Green Party Deserves a Spot on the Debate Stage," by Micaela Warren, *Daily Orange.* Reprinted by permission.

We're in the middle of a close presidential race, and many Americans are unhappy with their party's nominee—so much so that "settle for Biden" has become a trend on social media. Around 40% of Americans want a third party, according to a poll by CNN.

Both campaigns are trying to appeal to people who aren't voting because they don't feel compelled to by any candidate. It's possible that a third party could represent Americans better and make them get out and vote. But unfortunately, third parties in the United States aren't given a fair chance to represent the American people.

The 2020 election is not the first time third-party candidates' inability to participate in presidential debates has sparked outrage. Jill Stein, the nominee for the Green Party, and Gary Johnson, the Libertarian Party nominee, did not qualify to be in any of the presidential debates in 2016. Stein took a more aggressive stance by asking supporters to get her onto the debate stage without being invited by the commission.

Now, Howie Hawkins, the 2020 Green Party presidential nominee, is lobbying for himself and all third-party nominees to be part of the last presidential debate of this year.

Hawkins, a Syracuse resident, has a long political history. He co-founded the Green Party in 1984 and is an environmentalist. He received the Green Party's nomination in July and picked Angela Walker, a professional environmental activist, to be his running mate. She's described on her campaign website as "A fierce advocate for the rights of Black, Brown and Indigenous people, the LGBTQIA community, Labor and the Earth itself."

These are issues our politicians in power need to address right now. Both Hawkins and Walker could be the change we need in America, but they are being unrightfully silenced.

The Green Party of New York describes itself as social justice advocates, grassroots activists and environmentalists.

"Government must be part of the solution, but when it's controlled by the 1%, it's part of the problem," the party's website states. Many Americans would agree with the removal of billionaires and capitalism in politics.

Pew Research Center found in 2018 that 77% of Americans believe there should be a limit on campaign spending. This might level the playing field for politicians who don't take money from big donors.

We see this in both the way President Donald Trump and former Vice President Joe Biden conduct themselves in interviews and speeches. Trump is frequently heard saying "drain the swamp," in reference to corruption in politics. Biden has been adamant about saying he's taking small, grassroots donations over billionaires' money.

The Green Party is proposing necessary changes to the way Americans live. The party focuses on inclusivity and building an environmentally-aware world.

The Green Party could be mistaken for having similar ideas to the Democratic Party, but its website draws clear distinctions. The party's website goes after Democrats for not being set enough on their issues, often calling them out for "lukewarm support" of topics such as abortion rights.

Hawkins, Walker and the Green Party also stand strong on issues related to gender equality. With the possible confirmation of Amy Coney Barrett to the Supreme Court and recent concerns about her stance on *Roe v. Wade*, gender equality is an issue on the forefront of many Americans' minds.

If the Green Party is accurately representing the American people in a way that Democratic and Republican nominees are not, what is the harm of letting them debate? Third-party candidates deserve a chance to pull votes from the Democratic or Republican Party, and the American people should have a chance to hear what they have to say. Third parties belong on the debate stage.

| *"As climate change becomes a major— if not the major—voting issue for young people, why isn't the Green Party growing as a political force?"*

# Greens Aren't Getting Their Message Out

*Rainesford Stauffer*

*In the following viewpoint, Rainesford Stauffer argues that many young people are concerned about climate change, yet few are joining the Green Party. Once an issue gains importance, major parties often address it. That can mean young voters don't see much difference between the Green Party and the Democratic Party when it comes to the environment. Because the US election system is heavily weighted in favor of the two major parties, voting for a third party can feel like throwing away a vote. The question becomes, can the Green Party share its message in a way that appeals to more voters? Rainesford Stauffer has written and reported for the* New York Times, WSJ Magazine, Teen Vogue, Vox, *and* The Atlantic, *among other outlets.*

As you read, consider the following questions:

1. How does the Green Party support younger voters?
2. How can young people promote their political views?
3. How is climate change connected to other social and political issues?

"Why Young People Worried About Climate Change Aren't Joining the Green Party," by Rainesford Stauffer, *Teen Vogue*, October 4, 2019. Reprinted by permission.

For 15-year-old Kentucky activist Lily Gardner, the 2018 midterms were the first time she saw politicians dig in on an issue she thinks is of paramount importance: climate change. According to Lily, she's one of the first Appalachian members of the Sunrise Movement, and she looked on excitedly as progressive advocates for fighting the climate crisis, including Alexandria Ocasio-Cortez and Ilhan Omar, were elected to office.

Lily says she agrees with most of what she's seen from the Green Party over the last couple years, but she never considered aligning herself with the independent political party focused on a global green movement. "When climate change became a very big political priority for me, there were Democratic candidates who were there proposing the solutions that were the same as the Green Party's, frankly," Lily tells *Teen Vogue*.

Lily is just one example of an informed, engaged young climate activist who doesn't identify with the party that, on a base level, would seem most aligned with her interests. Millennials and Generation Z are most likely to see a link between human activity and climate change, and in a Harvard poll of voters between 18 and 29, 45% surveyed said they think climate change is an urgent crisis.

As climate change becomes a major—if not the major—voting issue for young people, why isn't the Green Party growing as a political force? As young climate activists and the Green New Deal, put forth by Representative Ocasio-Cortez and Senator Ed Markey, dominate headlines and encourage young voters to go to the polls, is the Green Party leveraging this surge of new energy?

"The reason the Green Party is at the periphery of American politics, and is likely to remain so for the foreseeable future, is that the United States is largely a two-party system," explains Jacob Neiheisel, associate professor in the department of political science at the University at Buffalo. "The low chance of success for third parties in legislative elections is further compounded by the fact that voters recognize the difficulties that third parties face and don't want to 'waste' their vote."

Neiheisel says that, historically speaking, when a third party advances a position that begins gaining momentum, major parties often take up that same position, while roadblocks like ballot access laws trip up third parties. "With the Democratic Party taking a stand on the issue of climate change that, at least for most members of the electorate, sounds similar to the position offered by the Green Party," he continues, "[so] there isn't much use in supporting a third party that has very little chance of success when a major party has more or less adopted the same position."

Maya Siegel, a 19-year-old climate activist, echoes that sentiment. "It doesn't feel like it would count as much if I voted for a candidate on the Green Party," explains Siegel, pointing out that in conversations with her peers, they'd found some ideas aspirational but not realistic, like cutting out single-use plastic when the substitutes are expensive. "For me, when I'm looking for a candidate, I want those bold, big ideas, but I also want realistic, small ideas along the way."

Lily mentions that the conversations she'd overheard about the Green Party while she was growing up were always dismissive. The adults she knew either never discussed the party in a serious manner, or, in the 2016 presidential election, blamed Jill Stein for taking votes away from more viable Democratic candidates.

Still, this moment of political unrest and environmental upset would seem like the right time for the Green Party to try to engage swaths of young and future voters. "The idea of there only being 'two parties' has been pushed by the media for years as a way to suppress other parties," Ashley Frame, cochair of the National Green Party US Youth Caucus, tells *Teen Vogue*. Frame says that the Green Party Youth Caucus, the Young EcoSocialists, have their own 35-and-under delegates who vote on internal party matters at a national level as representatives of their generation, something she says wouldn't be an option in the Democratic and Republican parties. "I wouldn't say we are 'remaining small' when we are continuously growing," she adds. (The Green Party declined to provide specific figures on party membership.)

Frame says the Green New Deal, which a survey earlier this year found was supported by 59% of US voters, was first introduced about a decade ago, by the Green Party. "If they had listened to us then, we may actually have the Green New Deal in effect now," says Frame. "We don't just fit into the conversation of climate change; we define it."

But the conversation and voices are fundamentally shifting, as young people tired of waiting for politicians to take action on the issue that threatens their future start movements of their own. Swedish activist Greta Thunberg's international Fridays for Future school strikes, Zero Hour, and Sunrise Movement, all headed by young people, have demonstrated a fierce tenacity on an issue

## THE GREEN PARTY'S PLEDGE TO SOCIAL JUSTICE

We assert that the key to social justice is the equitable distribution of social and natural resources, both locally and globally, to meet basic human needs unconditionally, and to ensure that all citizens have full opportunities for personal and social development.

We declare that there is no social justice without environmental justice, and no environmental justice without social justice.

This requires:

- a just organization of the world and a stable world economy that will close the widening gap between rich and poor, both within and between countries; balance the flow of resources from South to North; and lift the burden of debt on poor countries that prevents their development.
- the eradication of poverty, as an ethical, social, economic, and ecological imperative
- the elimination of illiteracy
- a new vision of citizenship built on equal rights for all individuals regardless of gender, race, age, religion, class, ethnic or national origin, sexual orientation, disability, wealth or health

"Social Justice," Green Party of Canada Fund.

that also encompasses a housing crisis, health care crisis, and an economic crisis.

Rhiana Gunn-Wright, the policy lead for the Green New Deal at New Consensus, a think tank focused on implementing the sweeping plan, says the version of the policy that Jill Stein ran on in 2016 didn't look quite like the version we've since come to know.

Gunn-Wright says that the current version of the Green New Deal has been imagined from the "perspective of a young person, in the sense that the decisions that we make right now are going to shape so much of what happens for the next 50 years." She explains that the future orientation allows for something that's been missing from national discourse: what a future could look like after we band together to tackle climate change.

For young activists like Lily Gardner, part of the growing awareness around the climate crisis is that it is also a housing crisis and a health care crisis; it is an intersectional, all-encompassing issue touching on so many of our social and political functions as a country. "That was never something I thought the Green Party had made clear when they were the first people who were out there about climate change," she says. (The Green Party maintains this is part of their messaging.)

The messaging matters, according to Dr. Stephen Axon, an assistant professor of geography at Southern Connecticut State University and a climate justice activist. "It's almost paradoxical that given the number of people that are becoming further engaged with the issue of climate change that the Green Party is not a bigger force for change," he says, adding that it appears the Green Party has almost been "pigeonholed" in the US into a single-issue party, and that it's seen as taking votes from Democrats. He cites the Green parties of Europe and the U.K. as examples of how the party has gained traction in other places.

It's a framing issue, he says, because there are almost no identifiable Green Party politicians who have connected with voters in a widespread way. Meanwhile, a new wave of Democrats is espousing policy positions similar to the traditional Green Party platform. "The rhetoric of climate change has changed. It's not 'climate change,' it's the 'climate crisis,'" Axon continues. "Our climate is breaking down. Yet the Green Party is not front and center with this new language. It's the Democrats who are taking this forward, using it as a platform, and are engaging voters."

Axon believes having a Green Party is a plus because their progressive positions do shape people's perspectives. But recent worldwide climate strikes and local declarations of climate emergencies in places like Iowa City, Iowa, and Austin, Texas, have provided fresh evidence that this issue is already a pressing concern for many Americans. "It's just the Green Party is not leading on this front," Axon says.

Some young activists, like Lily, question whether the Green Party can ever be relevant at a moment when activists are calling for Democrats to hold a climate-specific presidential debate. In other words, has the new widespread focus on the climate crisis made it unnecessary to have a single party focused on the issue? Lily suggests that the Green Party itself may be "antiquated because climate change now needs to be the focus of so much of our government."

> "Our job in this country is also to educate people about what socialism is, how it improves people's material conditions, and how we can align it with the needs of the planet."

# The Green Party Deserves a Voice

*Joni Hess*

*In the following viewpoint, Joni Hess argues that many people probably would be interested in Green Party values, yet people don't know about the candidates. The current political system keeps third-party candidates off many election ballots. The media often doesn't report on third-party candidates. The major parties get the most money from special interest groups, and in turn their politicians push through laws that benefit those groups, the author claims. Joni Hess is a freelance journalist and fellow with openDemocracy's 50.50 section.*

As you read, consider the following questions:

1. Why do so few Americans know about the Green Party's proposals, according to the author?
2. In what way isn't the media doing its job, according to the source quoted?
3. How do special interest groups influence politics?

"'Stop Voting from a Place of Fear'—the Other Candidates Deserve a Hearing," by Joni Hess, Open Democracy, November 2, 2020. Reprinted by permission.

Which candidates are actually talking about measures that will change the system that enables police to continually murder Black people and other people of colour with impunity? The system, this system, is inherently flawed. And we are the only party talking about that."

That's Angela Walker, Green Party candidate for vice-president. She's on the ticket in thirty states, yet most voters have never heard her name.

They haven't heard of her running-mate, Howie Hawkins, either. "The campaign that Angela and I are running on," he says, "according to public opinion polling, is the most popular platform. People want a Green New Deal. They want Medicare for All. They want the cancellation of student debt and free tuition at public colleges and universities. They want to get out of these endless wars."

Many of their ideas on climate change follow the lead of top researchers, scientists and the United Nations. But they are treated as marginal.

Talking to me ahead of a rally in Minneapolis, Libertarian candidate Jo Jorgensen is caustic about Trump and Biden. "Neither one has an answer to the question of healthcare costs, and neither one is going to bring the troops home. So a lot of voters have been saying to me, it's nice to have somebody that I can actually vote for, rather than against."

But despite expressing popular sentiments, despite echoing the views of people I speak to in New Orleans, where I live, or on a recent trip to Kentucky, in the US electoral system, these are fringe candidates.

Many of the people I've spoken to don't talk about ideas for how to invest in the sustainability of the planet, their health and their communities. Instead, they tend to talk about their fears.

And for Walker this is how the Democrats and Republicans retain their grip, "Stop voting from a place of fear... How about we look forward to what it is we actually want, the kind of country we actually want to live in?"

## Broken Politics

The US political system places numerous blocks between third-party candidates and voters.

"Ballot access is a huge issue" says Hawkins, describing how he spent a month campaigning in Pennsylvania only for the Democrats to succeed in getting him struck off the ballot, because a Green Party official had sent documents in separate envelopes rather than together. "In New York, we need 3,500 signatures. We had six weeks to collect them. In Indiana, over 40,000." In the UK, he points out, each candidate for Parliament needs just ten. In India, it's two.

Jorgensen managed to get on the ballot in every state, but believes the media plays a huge role in preserving the two-party system. "Having a third person on the ballot in all fifty states who every single American in this country can vote for and they're not reporting on it. I would say they aren't doing their job."

## Dark Money

Greens and Libertarians agree that fighting the amount of corporate money funneled into politics is an uphill battle. "Corporations will actually write the law, hand it to a congressperson, and the congressperson introduces it as a bill," said Jorgensen.

An investigation by the Center of Public integrity in 2018 revealed that these "model laws" push an agenda by special interest groups including limiting access to abortion and the rights of protesters. By pushing these laws through, politicians make friends who in return will donate to their campaigns in the future.

For the Greens, the solution is "full public campaign finance, on the clean money model," explains Hawkins. "They do this in Arizona and in Maine for state elections…. You qualify by getting a reasonable number of small $5 donations, then you run on public money, not private money."

Candidates like Hawkins and Jorgensen are keenly aware of what they're up against. They aren't running to win this year's election (although they'll never openly admit to that). They're in it for the long game and are relying on Americans to think in terms of what they need instead of settling for the lesser of two evils. "When they go to the polls, I hope every American realises and values the freedom we have in this country that we're slowly turning over to the people in Washington," said Jorgensen.

## "I Don't Do Smoke and Mirrors: I'm a Socialist"

Greens and Libertarians agree that America's political system is broken. They agree that America needs to end its foreign wars. But their domestic solutions are radically different.

"I don't do smoke and mirrors. I am a socialist," says Walker. "Black people in this country have a very proud history of being socialist. I know that they've been using "socialist" as a curse word to hit each other back and forth. And you know, all we do is laugh: I mean, you want to talk to some socialists, we right here!

"Our job in this country is also to educate people about what socialism is, how it improves people's material conditions, and how we can align it with the needs of the planet."

Jorgensen has a very different perspective. For her, the problem is an overweening state. When I ask her if she supports the Black Lives Matter call to defund the police, for example, she replies: "Crime is a local issue. I would allow each different jurisdiction to decide how they want to handle their policing. And I would absolutely end giving tanks and tear gas and grenade launchers to the over 8,000 federal state and local police forces.

"If you're sitting in Austin, Texas, or Albuquerque, New Mexico or Charleston, West Virginia, and they put a referendum on the ballot: 'Would you like your taxes raised so that our police department can go out and buy a tank?' most people would say: 'No, I'd rather keep that extra money, maybe walk to a nice dinner or go to a nicer vacation.'

"But what happens is the federal government takes that money from us, then they buy the tanks and tear gas. And then they dangle it in front of the police department. So that 'OK, do you want a free tank?'"

If the polls are right, Biden is going to be the US president. The system will hold itself together. For now. But anyone who can smell the air can tell that something is going to break.

# Periodical and Internet Sources Bibliography

*The following articles have been selected to supplement the diverse views presented in this chapter.*

Ballotpedia, "List of Political Parties in the United States," https://ballotpedia.org/List_of_political_parties_in_the_United_States

Rob Garver, "'Third Party' Threat to the Status Quo of US Politics Faces Long Odds," VOA News, May 18, 2021. https://www.voanews.com/usa/us-politics/third-party-threat-status-quo-us-politics-faces-long-odds

Maggie Haberman, Danny Hakim, and Nick Corasaniti, "How Republicans Are Trying to Use the Green Party to Their Advantage," September 22, 2020. https://www.nytimes.com/2020/09/22/us/politics/green-party-republicans-hawkins.html

Jeffrey M. Jones, "Support for Third US Political Party at High Point," Gallup, February 15, 2021. https://news.gallup.com/poll/329639/support-third-political-party-high-point.aspx

Khan Academy, "Third-Party Politics: Lesson Overview." https://www.khanacademy.org/humanities/us-government-and-civics/us-gov-political-participation/us-gov-third-party-politics/a/lesson-summary-third-party-politics

Lawrence Lessig, "Third Parties Fear the Democrats' Big Voter Bill. It'll Actually Help Them," *Washington Post*, March 16, 2021. https://www.washingtonpost.com/outlook/2021/03/16/hr1-public-funding-third-parties/

Lumen Learning, "Minor Political Parties." https://courses.lumenlearning.com/boundless-politicalscience/chapter/minor-political-parties/

Stuart Parker, "It's Time to Put the Green Party Out of Its Misery," RealClearEnergy, September 21, 2020. https://www.realclearenergy.org/2016/10/24/why_is_the_us_green_party_so_irrelevant_279481.html

Pew Research Center, "Political Party Quiz." https://www.pewresearch.org/politics/quiz/political-party-quiz/

Kevin Reed, "Democrats Engineer Removal of Green Party Presidential Candidates from Pennsylvania Ballot," World Socialist Web Site, September 18, 2020. https://www.wsws.org/en /articles/2020/09/18/penn-s18.html

Brian Schwartz, "Total 2020 Election Spending to Hit Nearly $14 Billion, More Than Double 2016's Sum," CNBC, October 28, 2020. https://www.cnbc.com/2020/10/28/2020-election -spending-to-hit-nearly-14-billion-a-record.html

Patrick Strickland, "For Some on the US Left, Green Party Is a Strategic Vote," Al Jazeera, November 8, 2016. https://www .aljazeera.com/features/2016/11/8/for-some-on-the-us-left -green-party-is-a-strategic-vote

Ethan Wollins, "People Must Only Consider Republican or Democratic Candidates for November Elections," *Badger Herald*, September 28, 2020. https://badgerherald.com /opinion/2020/09/28/people-must-only-consider-republican-or -democratic-candidates-for-november-elections/

Xinhua, "US Third-Party Candidate Fights for Party's Survival, Urging Election Reform," November 11, 2020. http://www .xinhuanet.com/english/2020-11/03/c_139487955.htm

OPPOSING
VIEWPOINTS®
SERIES

# CHAPTER 4

# Can Green Politics Become Relevant in America?

# Chapter Preface

P revious chapters showed the challenges the Green Party, and other smaller parties, face in America. In US elections, the candidate with the most votes wins (in presidential elections, it's the most Electoral College votes), even if they only had a few more votes than the second-place candidate. This has given America a two-party system, where the Republicans and Democrats fight for power. Voting for a third party is often seen as taking away votes from one of those major parties.

Some European democracies use proportional representation. This means political parties win seats in elections based on the percentage of voters who support them. If a party wins a quarter of the popular vote, it will hold roughly a quarter of the seats in the government after the election. Small parties can have a voice and build power over time, especially if they work together or with a major party.

Replacing the current system with proportional representation would allow smaller parties to have a voice. Those smaller parties could then attract more donations. The media would pay more attention to them. However, this would require replacing America's Electoral College system. Major changes seems unlikely to happen with two powerful parties wanting to maintain their advantage. Still, perhaps the Green Party could build power over time, by starting at the local level. Or perhaps the party is already doing valuable work by starting new conversations about its ideals.

Any large group is made up of thousands of individuals, which makes for a variety of opinions on how the Green Party should face the future. Some say compromise is important in building coalitions with other political parties. Others say the Green Party should go back to the purity of its environmental vision. Yet others say the party should reach out to people from more diverse backgrounds. This chapter explores what might need to happen for the Green Party to become more relevant in America.

| "The United States' archaic winner-take-all voting system allows the candidate with the most votes to win the whole election, even if he or she does not win a majority of the votes."

# The United States Needs More Than Two Political Parties

*Kristin Eberhard*

*In the following excerpted viewpoint, Kristin Eberhard argues that having only two major political parties in the United States does not reflect the values and priorities of the entire population. In fact, the author notes, the number of self-identified independent voters in the United States is rising, particularly in the millennial generation. The current system results in dissatisfied voters, politicians who can't keep their promises, legislative gridlock, and polarization. Kristin Eberhard is a researcher, writer, speaker, lawyer, and policy analyst who spearheads Sightline Institute's work on democracy reform and on climate action. She is the author of the book* Becoming a Democracy: How We Can Fix the Electoral College, Gerrymandering, and Our Elections.

"The United States Needs More Than Two Political Parties," by Kristin Eberhard, Sightline, April 28, 2016. Reprinted by permission.

As you read, consider the following questions:

1. According to the viewpoint, what percentage of American voters identify as independent?
2. What is winner-take-all voting?
3. How is gerrymandering fueled by winner-take-all, according to the author?

I want a political party that represents my views. Like many Oregonians, Washingtonians, and a growing number of Americans, I'm not a Democrat, and I'm not a Republican.

Independents—people who don't identify with one of the two major parties—are the biggest and fastest-growing group of US voters. At last count, 40 percent of Americans considered themselves independent. The same is true in Cascadia: in Washington, an estimated 44 percent of registered voters identify as independent; in Oregon, one-third of registered voters are not registered Democrat or Republican. The trend is even more stark among younger Americans: nearly half of millennials consider themselves independent.

Yet Cascadians who live in the United States are continually shoe-horned into the two major parties because, like Richard Gere in *An Officer and a Gentleman*, we've got nowhere else to go.

## More Parties Would Better Represent Voters' Views

The growing number of Americans who don't identify with either major party and the surprising popularity of party-outsiders Sanders and Trump indicate Americans want options outside the two major parties. Two parties can adequately represent people's views along a single axis, but when views bifurcate along two different axes, two parties cannot reflect the diversity of political views. American voters span a spectrum from progressive to conservative on a left-right cultural axis, and they span a spectrum from elitist to populist on an up-down economic axis. (I use the term "elitist" for lack of a better term: it represents a preference for policies that benefit the economic elite, including corporations, financial institutions, and the wealthy. Economic elitists tend to oppose policies that distribute economic benefits to working- or middle-class people, like Social Security, taxes on wealth or capital gains, limits on "free trade" to protect domestic blue-collar jobs at the expense of corporate profit, and prioritizing domestic spending that may benefit Americans broadly over international interventions that may benefit corporations.)

Using data from the Pew Research Center's 2014 Political Typology Report, I charted seven of Pew's political typologies left to right—progressive to conservative—and top to bottom—economic elitist to economic populist. This two-axis analysis suggested several points:

- Culturally conservative and economically elitist Americans, the "Business Conservatives" in the upper right quadrant, feel at home in the Republican party. However, business elites are worried that rising populist sentiments may hurt their bottom line, and the elitist GOP establishment is horrified that an uncouth populist like Trump is laying claim to its party banner.
- Culturally conservative and economically populist voters, the "Steadfast Conservatives" in the lower right quadrant, are relatively satisfied with the Republican party's cultural conservatism but may feel alienated from the Republican party's elitist economic policies. It follows that many of these voters are thrilled to hear Trump trumpet a culturally conservative worldview while also expressing populist economic messages, like limiting free trade and spending taxpayer dollars solving problems at home—not playing world police. Many Trump supporters also favor increasing taxes on the wealthy.
- Culturally moderate and economically populist voters, the "Young Outsiders" and the "Hard-Pressed Skeptics" in the lower middle quadrant, are dissatisfied with both parties, possibly because both parties are too focused on cultural

issues rather than economic populism. Many of these voters are delighted to hear Sanders hammer on wealth inequality, financial access to college, a living wage, limiting free trade, and solving economic problems at home rather than paying to play world police.

- Culturally progressive and economically moderate Americans—"Faith and Family Left," "Next Generation Left," and "Solid Liberals" in lower left quadrant—feel pretty happy with the Democratic party. But the Democratic establishment is uncomfortable with Sanders' strident populism.

## THIRD-PARTY CANDIDATES

The United States has been a two-party system since its creation, yet today there are multiple third-party candidates on voting ballots. In presidential elections the US has never seen a third-party candidate win, but every election they remain an option for voters. Professionals at the University of Minnesota Duluth examine why third-party candidates exist in today's elections.

The history of third-party candidates dates back to 1788. Even with the extensive history of third-party candidates, only four since 1920 have been able to win a single electoral college vote in the presidential election.

"Third-party candidates in the United States political system, the odds of them winning are really kind of remote, particularly at the presidential level," Cynthia Rugeley, the department head of the University of Minnesota Duluth's political science program said.

According to Rugeley, because third-party candidates usually never win a presidential election, their main purpose has turned into providing protest votes to people who don't believe in the two-party system.

Another purpose for third-party votes could be efforts to take votes away from either the Democratic or Republican parties.

**"Third-Party Candidates: Are They Worth It?" by Madison Hunter, The Bark, November 3, 2020.**

For the parties to maintain control of their banners and for more voters to see candidates they can get excited about, the United States needs parties that represent more of this diversity of views.

## Winner-Take-All Voting Suppresses Third Parties

The United States' archaic winner-take-all voting system allows the candidate with the most votes to win the whole election, even if he or she does not win a majority of the votes. Third-party candidates are almost always doomed to fail, either to become "spoilers" who hand the election to the less popular of the two major party candidates (Nader spoiled it for Gore, Perot spoiled it for Bush) or else to get weeded out in top-two primaries like Washington's.

Bernie Sanders and Donald Trump understand the constraints of the winner-take-all system. Sanders, an Independent-Socialist-Democrat, and Trump, an Independent-Democrat-unaffiliated-Republican, figured the odds of successfully infiltrating a major party's primaries were higher than the odds of successfully running as third-party candidates. The popularity of party-outsiders Sanders and Trump shows voters are looking for views outside the two major parties' orthodoxies. But when the voting system works against third parties, third-party candidates can't win, third parties can't grow, and voters who prefer third parties can't vote their conscience without feeling like they are throwing away their votes.

Many Oregonians (including yours truly) are members of the Independent Party of Oregon: enough of us that the state awarded us major party status last year. But despite our numbers, winner-take-all voting prevents independents from winning elections in part because voters are afraid to spoil the election for their preferred Democrat or Republican candidate. Practicality propels us to keep voting for the Democrat or the Republican. Independent voters are barred from even voting in May's closed presidential primaries unless we defect and register as Democrats or Republicans.

In most stable Western democracies, Sanders and Trump wouldn't have to foist themselves on hostile parties; they could just run on their own parties' platforms. Simple. Most Western democracies use a form of voting that enables three or four viable parties. Of the 34 OECD countries, only the United Kingdom and its former colonies Canada and the United States still use winner-take-all voting—an eighteenth-century system that enables two parties to disproportionately dominate elections. Almost all other prosperous democracies use some form of proportional representation—a twentieth-century voting systems that enable multiple parties to accurately represent voters' views.

Yet even there, the wildly unrepresentative 2015 UK election results stirred calls for adopting a more modern voting system, and Canada has vowed that 2015 will be the last first-past-the-post election it ever holds. In 1996, New Zealand broke its eighteenth-century English winner-take-all voting bondage and adopted twentieth-century proportional representation voting, immediately adding several viable parties and making the legislature represent the full range of voters.

It is time for the United States to join the civilized world and shed its archaic voting system. The Cascadian parts of the country, especially Oregon and Washington, could lead the way, as I will detail in my next article.

## Proportional Representation Voting Enables Multiple Parties

Robert Reich envisions rising economic populism manifesting itself as a new "People's Party." While he is right that many people on both sides of the left-right divide are desperate for more economically populist candidates, he is, sadly, wrong that America will create a viable additional party just because lots of people really, really want one (or two).

If really wanting were enough, the United States would have created more viable parties during the Progressive Era. If wanting were enough, Ross Perot's Reform Party would still be around.

The paucity of parties stems not from a lack of interest but from a lack of a modern voting system. Until the United States updates how it votes, American voters will only have two viable options on their ballots, no matter how many people click their heels and wish it weren't so.

By design, winner-take-all voting disproportionately advantages two major parties, while proportional representation voting empowers parties in proportion to how many voters their platforms actually represent.

## The Example of New Zealand

New Zealand used winner-take-all voting for most of the twentieth century, and two major parties, National (conservative) and Labor (progressive), consistently won almost all the seats. Since switching to proportional representation in 1996, the Green Party (progressive, environmental), the New Zealand First Party (centrist, populist, nationalist), and the Maori Party (representing indigenous people) have gained seats in Parliament proportional to the number of voters who support them (12 percent, 9 percent, and 2 percent, respectively).

## The Example of Canada

In Canada, thirteen commissions, assemblies, and reports over the years recommended proportional representation. But Canada continued to suffer disproportional elections: Stephen Harper and the Conservative Party ruled for nearly a decade even though only a plurality of voters (36 to 40 percent) voted for the Conservative Party. Conservatives formed a minority government with 36.3 percent of the votes in 2006, but won a majority 53.9 percent of the legislative seats in 2011 with just 39.6 percent of the votes.

In 2015, the Liberal Party and the progressive New Democratic Party (NDP) both campaigned on the promise to abolish first-past-the-post voting. The Liberal Party swept to power with 54.4 percent of the seats (but only 39.5 percent of the vote), while the NDP won 13 percent of the seats (with 19.7 percent of the vote). The

Liberal Party favors instant runoff voting (IRV), likely because it might let Liberals continue to win close to a majority of seats. The NDP favors proportional representation (specifically, a form called Mixed Member Proportional).

Prime Minister Trudeau has promised to form a multi-party committee to explore the question of which voting system is best. The NDP recommended that, in keeping with the spirit of the exercise, committee membership should be proportional to the parties' share of the vote in fall 2015: five Liberals, three Conservatives, two New Democrats, one Bloc Quebecois, and one Green.

## The US Opportunity

In the United States, hardly anyone even talks about the benefits of proportional representation. In 1967, the US Congress mandated single-member districts, foreclosing proportional representation at the federal level. Good news: there are no Constitutional barriers to repealing this law and replacing it with something like the Fair Representation Act. Bad news: passing such an act through Congress will be a hard slog. As with most important changes in the United States, national reform is a long road that starts with the states.

States can experiment and spread success. Oregon and Washington could implement proportional representation in state legislatures. As more states follow suit, a bevy of benefits would compound: more voters would gain experience electing representatives through proportional voting, viable parties would gain ground, Sanders and Trump supporters would grow accustomed to electing like-minded representatives at the state level, and Congress would feel the pressure to adopt, or at least allow, proportional voting at the national level. States could make the first inroads into reforming federal elections by creating an interstate compact for fair representation and taking it to Congress asking for permission.

## Proportional Representation Could Also Boost Civic Engagement, Cripple Gerrymandering, and End Partisan Gridlock

I am not constructing an elaborate ruse to bolster my pet political party. I am advocating to improve democracy in Cascadia so that Cascadians can make progress towards sustainability. Updating the US voting system to one that empowers more than two major parties would not only give me, other independents, and Sanders and Trump supporters a political home; it would convey copious other benefits.

As I have previously described in greater detail, winner-take-all voting yields negative campaigns that turn off voters. Because a candidate can win by gaining more support than the other guy, but not necessarily majority support, smearing an opponent, or even sullying the whole election process so that voters simply stay home on election day, can be a successful strategy. When voters have the option to more fully express their preferences because they can rank candidates or choose a party that more closely aligns with their views, candidates and parties are motivated to attract voters to their ideas, not to repel voters from their opponents or from participating in civic life at all.

In addition to encouraging negative campaigns, winner-take-all voting also discourages voters with disproportionate or unrepresentative election results. What's the point in voting when you can never actually elect someone who represents your views? Voters who prefer third-party candidates, conservative voters who live in urban areas, and progressive voters who live in rural areas face this disheartening situation every election: if you don't agree with the plurality of voters in your district then your vote doesn't matter. Proportional representation voting encourages voters by ensuring that every vote counts. Conservatives, progressives, and third-party enthusiasts can all elect legislators in proportion to their strength at the ballot box.

A winner-take-all system also fuels the gerrymandering blight that plagues the United States. Gerrymandering can only exist when single-winner districts lines can be drawn around a particular demographic of voters. With proportional representation, it doesn't matter who draws the district lines, because districts are multi-winner or are balanced by a regional or statewide vote that ensures proportional results no matter how or by whom the districts are drawn.

Winner-take-all voting and the resulting two dominant parties also jam the system with partisan gridlock. The two-party system often rewards legislators for being obstructionist and punishes them for forming inter-party alliances to get things done. With more parties, obstructionists would become irrelevant to the art of governing, which would be carried out by skilled deal-makers. For example, imagine the United States added two additional parties—a conservative populist party that would occupy the political space around where the "Steadfast Republicans" are located, and a moderate-progressive populist party near the "Hard-Pressed Skeptics" and "Young Outsiders." A single party could no longer shut down public functions by taking its toys and going home. The other three parties would work out solutions and ignore the obstructionists. The two populist parties and the Democrats might come together to bolster Social Security and install Universal Health Care. Or they might draw enough support from the Democrats and Republicans to ensure trade agreements include protections for the American middle class.

## The Question of Governmental Effectiveness

Conventional wisdom in the United States says that, while a multi-party system might be more representative of the people, additional accuracy comes at the cost of governmental effectiveness. In a two-party system, the thinking goes, the party in charge can get things done, but in a multi-party system the small factions would be constantly fighting and never accomplish anything. If Congress is gridlocked now with two parties, just imagine what it would be like with three or four!

Researcher Arend Lijphart conducted an exhaustive international study and found that multi-party systems are more effective at governing, maintaining rule of law, controlling corruption, reducing violence, and managing the economy—particularly minimizing inflation and unemployment while managing the economic pressures arising from economic globalization. His conclusion boils down to: good management requires a steady hand more than a strong hand. Two-party systems provide more of the latter with a strong, decisive, government, while more representative multi-party democracies provide more of the former with steady governance.

The party in charge in a two-party system can make decisions faster, but once the other party gains control it often abruptly reverses course, throwing things into disarray. And the ruling party often has a hard time implementing decisions that they made over the vehement objections of important sectors of society, since those sectors continue to oppose the outcome at every turn. A multi-party government may take longer to form the consensus needed to make a decision, but once made, decisions are durable, implementable, and not at constant risk of being overturned.

## Conclusion

A representative democracy means voters elect representatives who share their values, beliefs, and priorities. With more than one set of issues at stake, two political parties cannot possibly field candidates who reflect the different permutations of voters. The growing number of independent voters and the Sanders and Trump insurgencies demonstrate voters' discontent with the deficient representation that two major parties can offer. So while outsiders like Sanders and Trump may never win a single-winner seat like the presidency, with proportional voting, the many voters rallying to the Sanders and Trump flags could elect legislators in proportion to their numbers.

> "The GOP has a long history of using
> the Green Party as a tool to siphon
> votes that might go to Democrats
> and of playing a spoiler role in
> our two-party, winner-take-all
> electoral system."

# A Vote for the Green Party Only Helps the Republicans

*John Bachtell*

*In the 2020 US election, the Green Party tried to get on the ballot in several states. The Republican Party, sometimes called the GOP ("Grand Old Party"), supported the Green Party in some of these requests and the court cases that followed. In the following viewpoint, John Bachtell argues that the GOP used the Green Party to undermine the Democrats. According to the author, Republicans support putting Green Party candidates on ballots, knowing that Green votes will take votes away from Democrats. Fewer votes for Democrats means a greater likelihood the Republicans will win. John Bachtell is the publisher of* People's World, *a progressive news outlet. He served as chairman of the National Committee of the Communist Party USA from 2014 to 2019.*

"GOP Election Sabotage Scheme Using Wisconsin Green Party Stalls," by John Bachtell, Courtesy of *People's World*, September 17, 2020. Reprinted by permission.

As you read, consider the following questions:

1. What reason did the Wisconsin Supreme Court give for denying the Green Party's request to be on the ballot?
2. How can the Republican Party benefit when the Green Party gets on a ballot?
3. How does the current electoral system make voting for a third party a problem, according to the author?

The Wisconsin Supreme Court ruled Sept. 14 against placing the Green Party on the 2020 election ballot. The decision vacated a hold the same court had put on sending ballots to municipalities and 1 million absentee ballots to voters last week.

Under Wisconsin law, election officials must send more than a million requested mail-in ballots to voters by Sept. 17. The Help America Vote Act requires the state send ballots to military personnel by Sept. 24. Officials have already sent hundreds of ballots out in order to meet those deadlines. If the Greens had prevailed in their court case, the state would have had to re-print and re-send all new ballots to replace those already mailed, a process that could take weeks and cause voters to miss election mailing deadlines.

The Republican Party made no effort to hide its use of the Green Party's case in Wisconsin, a critical battleground state. The GOP directed the Greens' legal strategy, including supplying a GOP-linked law firm to argue the case and saw the scheme as an opportunity to draw votes away from Joe Biden and Kamala Harris.

By filing to put the Green Party on the ballot, the GOP hoped to create havoc with mail-in votes in Wisconsin that favor Democrats, similar to plots being carried out nationwide. It was another in a long list of efforts to sabotage balloting. A GOP effort to get rapper Kanye West on the ballot in Wisconsin to siphon African-American votes also failed. The GOP is still helping get West on the ballot in four other states.

In Wisconsin, nearly 80% of voters opted for mail-in ballots in the state's Aug. 11 primary election for state and local candidates. The Green Party delayed filing a complaint for two weeks after the State Elections Commission deadlocked over putting them on the ballot, thus raising questions about their true intent.

Despite the Republicans' brazenness, the Green Party leadership went along with the scheme anyway. "You get help where you can find it," the party's presidential candidate Howie Hawkins told the *Washington Post*. "They have their reasons, and we have ours." It was a GOP member of the State Election Commission that had referred the Greens to the GOP law firm that came to their aid.

The 4-3 majority on the state Supreme Court, which included GOP-aligned Justice Brian Hagedorn, acknowledged the 2020 elections "had already begun" and decided that redrawing the ballot at this late date would create enormous chaos. Reprinting ballots would force the state to miss critical deadlines to send out ballots and undermine confidence in the election outcome.

Wisconsin Democratic Party chair Ben Wikler called the ruling a "major victory for democracy" and said it would ensure safe voting options during the pandemic.

## Republican Tool

The GOP has a long history of using the Green Party as a tool to siphon votes that might go to Democrats and of playing a spoiler role in our two-party, winner-take-all electoral system. And the Green Party leadership has opportunistically embraced the support, playing the role of what some describe as "useful idiots." They consistently equate Democrats and Republicans as two corrupt capitalist parties irrespective of the two parties' social base and platform. Green leaders often even target Democrats as the greater evil.

In 2016, Green Party presidential candidate Jill Stein garnered 30,000 votes in Wisconsin; Trump won the state by 23,000 votes.

On Aug. 25, the US Supreme Court declined to hear an appeal from the Montana Secretary of State to restore the Green Party to the November ballot. There, the GOP engaged in what State Democratic Party Executive Director Sandi Luckey called "a massive fraudulent effort to mislead Montana voters and tamper with our elections."

The Montana GOP bankrolled the effort to get the Green Party on the ballot, including funding from a Texas right-wing group. When hundreds of people who had signed the petitions found out the Republican Party was behind the scam, they requested removing their signatures, leaving the Green Party short of the total they needed.

While Montana is not a presidential swing state, the GOP sought to influence a close US Senate race there that could potentially flip majority control of the chamber to Democrats and the House of Representatives race.

Other incidents of the GOP manipulatively using the Green Party include:

During the 2016 elections, Russian intelligence operatives funded a sophisticated and widespread social media campaign, including promoting Stein. Russian state television network Russia Today and the news agency Sputnik regularly broadcast coverage favorable to her candidacy, while Russian government-linked online outlets published at least 100 stories and articles promoting Stein. Overwhelming evidence exists of collusion between the Trump campaign and the Russian government in the 2016 elections.

In the 2000 elections, Green Party presidential candidate Ralph Nader practically threw Florida and New Hampshire to Republican George W. Bush. In Florida, Nader drew nearly 100,000 votes in a contest marred by fraud. The GOP-dominated US Supreme Court ultimately stepped in to stop the vote count, with Bush ahead by 537 votes. In New Hampshire, Nader drew 22,000 votes in, three times the winning margin.

In both 2000 and 2004, big Republican donors funded Nader television ads and targeted key battleground states in an attempt to drive votes away from Al Gore and John Kerry, respectively. In 2004, one in ten contributors to Ralph Nader's campaign was also a funder of the Bush/Cheney campaign.

Also in 2004, Republicans collected 40,000 signatures to get Nader on the Michigan ballot as an independent. Accusations of GOP infiltration of the Green Party also surfaced in Washington and elsewhere.

In 2006, GOP money went to Green Party Senate and House candidates in Pennsylvania. The Green Party Senate candidate openly admitted to being a spoiler candidate to siphon votes from Democratic candidate Bob Casey, Jr., who was seeking to unseat extreme right then-Sen. Rick Santorum. Casey ended up winning.

In 2012, the Texas GOP helped fund Green Party efforts to get their gubernatorial candidate to draw votes from Democrat Bill White and elect Rick Perry.

## A PATH TO THE PRESIDENCY

The Green Party is now on enough state ballots nationwide to receive 305 electoral votes in the 2020 election—270 are needed to win. This puts the Green Party on a potential path for success in the 2020 presidential election.

The news comes after the US District Court for the Northern District of Illinois made it easier for minor parties that were on the ballot in 2016 and 2018 to be granted ballot access for those same offices. The ruling comes in light of hardships that minor parties would face securing signatures on petitions during the COVID-19 outbreak.

The ruling granted the Green Party relief from ballot access petitioning requirements—this put the party on the general election ballot for major offices like the offices of president and vice president and US Senate.

The ruling stated that minor party candidates must obtain only 10 percent of the original petition requirements, with an extended deadline.

Howie Hawkins, who is currently leading in the primaries for the Green Party presidential nomination, is advocating for the Green Party to be on all ballots across the 50 states and D.C.

"Green Party Now Has Mathematically Possible Path to Presidency," by Jessica Barr, *Legislative Gazette*, April 28, 2020.

In 2018, a Green Party candidate for Congress, later discovered to be a GOP plant, ran against then-Rep. Chris Collins, R-N.Y., to siphon votes from a Democratic candidate. Collins won but later resigned in disgrace from Congress after being charged and then convicted of insider trading and lying to law enforcement officials.

## Paths to Real Political Independence

The grassroots base of Green Party voters is rightfully fed up with the political corruption of entrenched power and is motivated by the desire to bring about progressive change. They're looking for an option that is free of corporate influence, and they place their faith in a third party.

In many state and local races, election rules mean that going the route of third party or independent candidacies is a way to build progressive power and beat back political machines and pro-corporate office holders in the two major parties.

Nationally, though, so long as our two-party, winner-take-all electoral system exists, the Green Party or other third parties continue to be subject to manipulation to play a spoiler's role. A genuine people's third party, one that reflects a broad alliance of working-class and democratic forces, will only be possible with electoral law reform, including a parliamentary system as exists in Europe or ranked voting. Or when these forces act in unison to either create such a party or become the Democratic Party's dominant force.

Until that time, voting for a third party only helps to split the vote and aid the GOP.

"*The background to the Pennsylvania Green Party case is a revealing example of how ballot access requirements in states across the country are used by the two-party system as barriers to the participation of third parties.*"

# The Green Party Is Being Kept from Participating in Important Elections

*Kevin Reed*

*In the following excerpted viewpoint, Kevin Reed reports on a ruling by the Pennsylvania State Supreme Court ahead of the 2020 presidential election to exclude Green Party candidates from the ballot. Although the official reason was that the candidates' nominating petitions were insufficient, the author contends that the majority Democrat court blocked the Green Party candidates to avoid a repeat of the 2016 election, when the Democrat candidate failed to be elected. Some blame that result on votes for the Green Party candidate, which were perceived to have pulled voters away from Hillary Clinton, allowing Republican Donald Trump to win the presidency. Reed argues that this is a good example of why third parties will never be relevant on the national stage. Kevin Reed is a writer for the World Socialist Web Site and a member of the Socialist Equity Party.*

"Democrats Engineer Removal of Green Party Presidential Candidates from Pennsylvania Ballot," by Kevin Reed, World Socialist Web Site, September 18, 2020. Reprinted by permission.

As you read, consider the following questions:

1. How did the Republicans on Pennsylvania's State Supreme Court rule?
2. What was the paperwork error that got in the Green Party's way?
3. Who or what does the author blame for the monopoly of the two-party system?

In the second such action by a state court this week, the Pennsylvania state Supreme Court ruled Thursday the state could exclude Green Party candidates Howie Hawkins and Angela Walker from the ballot for the 2020 presidential elections.

In the 5-2 decision on partisan lines, the state supreme court overturned a lower court ruling that supported the Green Party against a decision by the Bureau of Elections to use an obscure technicality to throw out the nominating petitions that qualified their candidates for ballot status.

The ruling, which was endorsed by all five Democratic justices, states, "Because the procedures for nominating a candidate for office by nomination papers were not strictly followed here … the Secretary is directed to remove both candidates' names from the general election ballot." The two Republican judges said in a dissenting opinion they agree that the nominating petitions had been filed improperly but that the Green Party should be given the opportunity to fix their paperwork.

As was the case in the ruling by the Wisconsin state Supreme Court on Monday, the political purpose of the Pennsylvania ruling is to keep the Green Party from providing an alternative for voters who might otherwise cast ballots for Democrats Joe Biden and Kamala Harris.

In the 2016 election, Hillary Clinton lost to Donald Trump by 11,000 votes in Michigan, 23,000 in Wisconsin, and 44,000 in Pennsylvania. In each state, Green Party presidential candidate Jill Stein received more votes than Clinton's margin of defeat.

This led the Democrats, and their media apologists, to blame the Greens for a defeat which Clinton brought on herself by running a right-wing, anti-working-class campaign that allowed Trump to posture as the advocate of coal miners, steel workers, auto workers and others whose livelihood had been destroyed by the policies of big business and the Obama-Biden administration.

One conclusion drawn by the Democrats from the experience of 2016 was that the basic democratic right of third parties to ballot access and of the public to vote for a candidate of their choosing must not be allowed to disrupt the two-party system of Wall Street, the Pentagon and the CIA. Over the past two months, they have blocked the Green Party from obtaining ballot status in Wisconsin and Pennsylvania and the Socialist Equality Party from obtaining ballot status in Michigan—the same three states which were the margin of defeat for Clinton in the Electoral College.

While the World Socialist Web Site and the Socialist Equality Party—which is running its own candidates Joseph Kishore for US President and Norissa Santa Cruz for US Vice President—have fundamental class and political differences with the Green Party, we defend their right to participate in the 2020 elections. We denounce the Democratic Party for its repeated and blatant abuse of ballot access procedural rules and the courts to have Hawkins and Walker kicked off the November ballot.

The background to the Pennsylvania Green Party case is a revealing example of how ballot access requirements in states across the country are used by the two-party system as barriers to the participation of third parties and alternative candidates attempting to run in US federal elections.

The Green Party gathered signatures of registered voters on nominating petitions between March and August 2 of this year for a slate of five candidates for both federal and state offices. On August 3, Timothy Runkle, Green Party candidate for Treasurer of Pennsylvania, submitted 8,500 signatures—a minimum of 5,000 is required—to the Office of the Secretary of the Commonwealth in Harrisburg.

At the time that the petitioning began in March, the Green Party candidates for President and Vice President were Elizabeth Faye Scroggin and Neal Taylor Gaye, acting as stand-ins for the eventual nominees of a party convention, and these candidates' names were on the petitions submitted by Runkle to the state.

As the court ruling explains, Runkle's submission "included a notarized candidate affidavit for Howie Hawkins and a non-notarized affidavit for Angela Walker ('Candidates'), who were nominated as the Green Party's candidates for President and Vice President, respectively, at the national Green Party Convention on July 11, 2020."

On August 10, the Green Party filed two Substitute Nomination Certificates with the Secretary seeking to formally replace Scroggin and Gale with Hawkins and Walker. At this point everything seemed to be going according to established procedure and the Green Party would be on the ballot in November.

Then, in a well-worn pattern of political skullduggery, Democratic Party functionaries known as "Objectors" proceeded to file a petition in the Commonwealth Court, "to have the Green Party slate removed from the general election ballot based upon the presidential and vice presidential candidates' alleged failure to comply with the requirements of the Election Code pertaining to candidate affidavits and substitutions."

The Objectors then filed an application with the court on August 24 for "summary relief" seeking to strike the nominations of the five candidates and the two substitutions from ballots that would be printed and distributed within two weeks.

Among the claims that the Objectors presented as reasons that the Green Party candidates should not be granted ballot status were: "Scroggin's failure to affix her affidavit to the nominating paper," "she faxed a copy of her affidavit, sans cover letter or any other explanatory material, to a general fax number without notifying the Department or following up to ensure that it was obtained" and lack of an original "wet" signature on her affidavit.

However, the Commonwealth Court ruled in favor of the Green Party and said that the Objectors were attempting to "elevate form over substance" and that a "bureaucratic snafu" does not constitute "a fatal defect." The lower court also accepted the Green Party's argument that the Objectors, i.e., the Pennsylvania Democratic Party, were engaged in "distraction and spaghetti on the wall litigation tactics. It simply does not stick."

The appeal to the Pennsylvania Supreme Court was filed by Paul Stefano, a lawyer and Democratic Party Chairman from Lawrence County, and Tony C. Thomas, a Democratic Party activist from the Wilkes-Barre area.

Initially, in hearing the appeal, the Supreme Court halted the production of ballots throughout the state pending its decision. However, the Supreme Court majority ultimately overruled the Commonwealth Court's decision precisely on the basis of "bureaucratic snafu" considerations, writing, "that defect was fatal to Scroggin's nomination and, therefore, to Hawkins' substitution. Accordingly, the Secretary of the Commonwealth is directed to remove Howie Hawkins and Angela Walker from the general election ballot as the Green Party's nominees for President and Vice President."

There is near-unanimous support within the ruling political establishment for the attacks on basic electoral rights being carried out the both the Democrats and Republicans. In the ballot access lawsuit filed by the SEP in Michigan—which argued that the requirement to collect tens of thousands of signatures on petitions during the coronavirus pandemic was unconstitutional—judges appointed by both Republican and Democratic presidents came together with Michigan Democratic Governor Gretchen Whitmer to reject the case of the socialist candidates Kishore and Santa Cruz.

In an op-ed on Thursday, Gail Collins, a columnist for the *New York Times*, attacked all third-party candidates, defended the two-party system and expressed contempt for the rights of voters to choose an alternative. She wrote, "Throwing your support to a third-party candidate with no hope whatsoever of getting elected is, however, a good way to dodge responsibility."

Collins also repeated the well-worn lie that Green Party candidate Ralph Nader—who received nearly three million votes in the 2000 election, and nearly 100,000 in Florida alone—was responsible for the victory of Republican George W. Bush and defeat of Democrat Al Gore. The reality was that the Republican Party, with the support of the US Supreme Court, halted the recounting of ballots in Florida and gave the election to Bush without Gore and the Democrats mounting a political fight to stop it.

Both Bush and Trump won because of the anti-democratic character of the US political system, including the Electoral College itself, the two-party system, which limits "official" politics to the twin parties of Wall Street, and a host of restrictions on media coverage and political participation. Nader, for example, was denied the right to participate in presidential debates, despite his millions of supporters. It is the capitalist class, which ruthlessly enforces the two-party political monopoly, that is responsible for the reactionary consequences.

| "Hawkins believes many of his would-
be voters chose Biden simply to get
rid of Trump."

# It's Not Only About Winning Elections

*Abby Weiss*

*In the following viewpoint, Abby Weiss considers Green Party candidate Howie Hawkins's loss in the 2020 election. Hawkins had hoped the Green Party's presence would encourage Democratic and Republican candidates to address some issues they usually ignore. He also hopes the Green Party will be able to get more candidates in local elections. Finally, Hawkins believes young people will be more likely to support the Green Party as they become voters. Abby Weiss is digital managing editor of the* Daily Orange, Syracuse University's *independent student newspaper.*

As you read, consider the following questions:

1. Why does Hawkins feel many progressive voters will be disappointed in President Biden?
2. Why did the Green Party run a presidential campaign when it did not believe it could win?
3. How could today's teenagers help the Green Party in the future, according to the viewpoint?

"Howie Hawkins Unsurprised by Election Results, Hopeful for Green Party," by Abby Weiss, *Daily Orange*, November 2020. Reprinted by permission.

S yracuse presidential candidate Howie Hawkins expected the 2020 election to be a tough year for third parties. So when his Green Party campaign received less than 0.5% of the popular vote in New York state, he wasn't surprised.

"[In 2016], there was a lot of dissatisfaction with the candidates, and a lot of progressives wanted to cast a protest vote for the Green Party," Hawkins said. "But 2020 was a referendum on Trump."

Syracuse University College of Law alumnus and Democrat Joe Biden won the presidential election on Saturday after securing victories in key battleground states, including Pennsylvania and Michigan. President Donald Trump continues to falsely dispute the results of the election.

Hawkins, the co-founder of the Green Party and a retired UPS employee who lives in Syracuse, said he was in a meeting with his campaign team when he heard about Biden's victory. Unfazed by the news, he continued the meeting as normal.

This was Hawkins' 25th campaign—and loss—for public office.

"It really didn't divert us. We kept going through our agenda," he said. "By that point, we assumed it would be Biden in office."

Hawkins and his running mate, Angela Walker, received 0.2% of votes nationwide and 0.3 percent in New York, according to the Associated Press. The Green Party needed 130,000 votes or 2% of the total voter turnout in New York to appear on ballots in the state during next year's election, after the state passed a stricter ballot access law in April. The Green Party will have to secure 45,000 signatures to remain on the ballot.

The party used to need only 50,000 votes to stay on the ballot, which is significantly fewer votes than the current threshold, Hawkins said.

Hawkins received fewer votes this election than 2016 Green Party candidate Jill Stein, who won 1% of the popular vote that year.

Hawkins attributes the Green Party's losses in the 2020 election to two factors: a staunch commitment among progressives to remove Trump from office and the fact that Hawkins appeared on fewer ballots nationwide. The Green Party was on the ballot for 30 states this year, as opposed to 45 in 2016.

Hawkins believes many of his would-be voters chose Biden simply to get rid of Trump.

"Most progressives saw Biden as a vehicle to get rid of Trump, and Trump supporters saw Trump as a better guy for the economy," he said. "It wasn't about issues. It was all about Donald Trump, either for him or against him."

Hawkins believes Biden's moderate stance on some policy issues, as well as his efforts to appeal to conservative voters and politicians, will let down many progressive voters.

"A lot of progressives are going to be disappointed," he said. "A honeymoon will be short, and then a lot of people are going to be looking back at the Greens and what we're trying to do."

As part of his platform, Hawkins advocated for a federal plan to dramatically reduce greenhouse gas emissions, and an economic Bill of Rights, which would guarantee rights to employment, health care, affordable housing and a stable income.

When the Green Party needed a candidate, Hawkins agreed to run because he was one of the few candidates in his party with the experience to run a large-scale campaign, he said.

Hawkins said he doesn't plan to run for public office again, but may if party members ask him to. He would like to be a campaign manager for another party member.

"I have no definite plans," Hawkins said. "I never planned to run 25 times. It's really up to the Greens. I'm not saying no, but I'm not seeking anything. I'll be involved, but whether I'm a candidate or not remains to be seen."

Hawkins hopes to assist local Green Party candidates with their campaigns so that the party can gain ground through local elections. The main goal of Hawkins' presidential campaign was to encourage more Green Party candidates to run for local office and to put issues on the public agenda that Democratic and Republican candidates usually ignore.

By 2024, Hawkins hopes to have more Green Party representatives in local office and possibly in the state Legislature. After this year's election, he's more confident that a higher number of Green Party members will run for office, he said.

Hawkins said he has received many messages from young people encouraging members of the party to keep running for office.

"Young people see more clearly than older people, who have kind of resigned themselves to the fact that we don't have real solutions for the climate, in poverty, and economic opportunity in racism," Hawkins said. "People, particularly teenagers, say, 'Keep going, I want to vote for you, but I couldn't this time.' It just doubles your commitment when you hear all this encouragement."

"*The impact of this campaign will be felt for months and years to come in the form of new Green Party candidates from local and state office running and winning elections.*"

# Right Now, Awareness Is the Goal for the Green Party

*Ted Porath*

*In the following viewpoint, Ted Porath further explores how the Green Party can influence politics even if it does not actually win elections. The author unpacks the impact of Green Party candidate Jill Stein's run in the 2012 US presidential election, noting that though she didn't come close to winning, Stein may have served to change the dialogue and push Democrats to the left. Perhaps even more important, the viewpoint contends, is the impact of a candidate like Stein on state and local elections. Winning local elections could help the Green Party take power at the state level and eventually bring it to national prominence. Ted Porath is a journalist.* Isthmus *is an alternative newspaper based in Madison, Wisconsin.*

"Green Party Candidates Measure Success Not in Victories, But in Awareness," by Ted Porath, *Isthmus*, November 6, 2012. Reprinted by permission.

As you read, consider the following questions:

1. According to the viewpoint, why would a loss for a Green Party candidate not be a loss for the Green Party?
2. How can a third party influence the policies of major parties?
3. What does it mean to build a party from the bottom up?

For Democratic and Republican politicians, success is usually determined by winning the race. But when a political party knows it really has no chance of winning an election, it must measure success differently.

For the Green Party, success wasn't really measured by the 0.12% of the national vote that its 2008 presidential candidate, Cynthia McKinney, squeezed out. Beat out by money and name recognition, the Greens, as they call themselves, say they define "success" by expanding the political debates over its key environmental and grassroots issues and building party support over time.

This definition will more than likely come into play in Wisconsin in State Assembly District 78, where Green Party candidate Jonathan Dedering is running against incumbent Democrat Brett Hulsey. Last election cycle, Green candidate Ben Manski had a lot of success in his campaign against Rep. Hulsey, bringing in 31% of the vote. This is unlikely to be the case with Dedering, who has been unable to bring in the important endorsements and funds that Manski did in 2010.

Nonetheless, for some Green Party supporters in the area, like current Dane County Board Sup. Leland Pan, a loss for Dedering would not mean a loss for the party.

"In a lot of instances running for those seats has more to do with expanding the dialogue, raising awareness around certain issues, offering people a choice and raising awareness about third parties, than it does with actually winning the seat," Pan said. "Obviously there are some candidates that do have a shot of winning, like Ben, and I would obviously like to see Dedering win, but I think there are other benchmarks for success."

Dedering himself named not an election win, but party recognition in the Madison community and the building of activists for the group as a goal of his campaign.

"We need to keep pushing Green Party candidates in the city," Dedering said. "We really need to keep the party active in the city and give people an option to register their support of the party."

The same can be said for Greens on the national level with their presidential candidate, Dr. Jill Stein. Right from the beginning, it was clear that Stein was not going to be competitive in her race. However, for many of her supporters, Stein achieved success because she served as a vehicle to expose the weaknesses they saw in Obama's campaign. Many Greens felt that Obama had moved away from the liberal platform he ran on in 2008. By having Stein run a campaign around those issues, they hoped to push Obama back on the left track.

"Stein has been a success, I think, by drastically changing the dialogue," said Green Party student activist Damon Terrell. "She's elevated issues of student debt, single-payer healthcare and she's elevated issues of drone warfare. These are chinks in Obama's armor that are never going to be exposed from the right because their policies don't make any more sense. I think making Obama at least a moderate left-wing candidate would be nice."

Many Greens believe that Stein has been the most successful Green candidate to run since Ralph Nader, who got a record 2.7% of the popular vote in 2000. Stein is the first Green Party member to raise enough public dollars—$894,000 according to OpenSecrets .org—to receive federal matching funds. Because of this public support, Stein's campaign manager, Ben Manski, believes that she could move into the single digits in terms of percentage of the vote in this election. A CNN poll heading from October had Stein at 3% of the national vote.

"The impact of this campaign will be felt for months and years to come in the form of new Green Party candidates from local and state office running and winning elections," Manski said. "Jill Stein's run has already inspired literally millions of people to vote Green both in the presidential and local ticket races and certainly thousands of people to come into the party as activists and candidates."

Pan is hopeful that this can carry over into the Wisconsin political arena.

"I've seen that the Wisconsin Green Party has been re-energized by Jill Stein's campaign," Pan said. "They've been much more active than they have been. So, I hope that that continues beyond the presidential election. Then the Jill Stein campaign will have done its job in building these parties and building the Green Party up."

But the Greens may not be as effective as they hope, according to Prof. Donald Downs of the UW-Madison political science department. Downs thinks Green Party candidates might not be achieving their idea of success, locally or nationally.

"My guess is that the Green Party has not been all that effective," Downs said. "I think it's been under the radar and hasn't really gotten much notice."

> *"Given that serious action on climate will have to come out of the institutions we have—not those we might wish for—the strategies and tactics you are pursuing through the Green New Deal amount to political malpractice."*

# The Green New Deal Should Focus on Climate

*Jerry Taylor*

*In the following excerpted viewpoint, written in the form of an open letter to "Green New Dealers," Jerry Taylor implores supporters of the Green New Deal to rethink their strategy and focus on constructing a deal that might actually meet with success. The future of the planet depends on this, Taylor argues. The author contends that focusing on climate action legislation is more urgent and important, and that the non-climate socialist agenda currently included in the Green New Deal can wait. Jerry Taylor is an environmental activist and president of the Niskanen Center. Over the past two decades, Taylor has been one of the most prominent and influential libertarian voices in energy policy in Washington.*

"An Open Letter to Green New Dealers," by Jerry Taylor, Niskanen Center, March 31, 2019, https://www.niskanencenter.org/an-open-letter-to-green-new-dealers/. Licensed under CC BY 4.0 International.

As you read, consider the following questions:

1. What is one example of the non-climate-related goals the Green New Deal resolution calls for?
2. What does the author mean by "political watermelon"?
3. Why does the author reference the government's experience of reforming health care?

An Open Letter to Green New Dealers,

I write this as a friend who wants your movement to succeed. Your cause is just and, due to decades worth of political inaction (some of which, I'm sorry to say, I have to personally account for), the hour is late. As the U.N.'s sixth Global Environmental Outlook declared this month, "urgent action at an unprecedented scale" is necessary to address climate change and the degradation of critically important ecosystems. The 2019 Global Risks Report, published by the World Economic Forum (an international, nonprofit institute serving as a forum for top business, political, and academic elites from around the world), concludes that climate-related risks now account for three of the top five global risks by likelihood, and four of the top five by impact. While there is a wide distribution of possible outcomes from climate change, we are already incurring serious risks from existing greenhouse gas concentrations, and the most likely outcomes by 2100 (imperfectly and conservatively accounted for by the U.N. Intergovernmental Panel on Climate Change, otherwise known as the IPCC) are frightening. The worst-case scenarios—many of which are as likely to occur as the best-case scenarios—suggest that catastrophic tipping points might be crossed before we realize it, with the real possibility of severe and irreversible ecological, economic, and human damage if we fail to act.

You are right: It is long past time to mince words about the risks at our doorstep. Our cavalier attitude towards the well-being of future generations is ethically scandalous. We are playing a reckless game of dice with the future of the human race. Your movement, while sometimes given to overstatement regarding the certainty that apocalypse is now (or soon-to-be) upon us, sees past the hand-waving (hand-waving that is rebutted well, incidentally, by the website Skeptical Science and my colleague Joseph Majkut) and the shrugging ambivalence of many others. You are passionately animated by a full appreciation of what's at stake, and few are.

I worry, however, that despite all of the new energy you've unleashed on the political scene, you are setting your cause back, not moving it forward. Nothing about the seriousness of the threat we are facing changes the fact that politics is "the art of the possible," not exhortation for the impossible. Given that serious action on climate will have to come out of the institutions we have—not those we might wish for—the strategies and tactics you are pursuing through the Green New Deal amount to political malpractice. Moreover, the policy initiatives you're promoting are rightly difficult for political actors to swallow. As veteran Democratic operative Stuart Eizenstat warned this month, "Speaking from experience, by demanding the moon, their proposals will crash on the launching pad and lead to nowhere good."

## Wishing for Ponies

What makes your Green New Deal innovative is that it ties climate action to a host of extremely ambitious progressive initiatives that have little or nothing to do with climate change. The Green New Deal resolution (introduced in the House by Rep. Alexandria Ocasio-Cortez of New York's 14th district and in the Senate by Ed Markey of Massachusetts) is literally 10-parts "New Deal" to 1-part "climate." Beyond the climate-related goals it asks Congress to adopt, the resolution also calls for:

- "guaranteeing a job with a family-sustaining wage, adequate family and medical leave, paid vacations, and retirement security to all people of the United States,

- "strengthening and protecting the right of all workers to organize, unionize, and collectively bargain free of coercion, intimidation, and harassment,
- "strengthening and enforcing labor, workplace health and safety, antidiscrimination, and wage and hour standards across all employers, industries, and sectors,
- "ensuring a commercial environment where every businessperson is free from unfair competition and domination by domestic or international monopolies,
- "providing all people of the United States with high-quality health care,
- "providing all people of the United States with affordable, safe, and adequate housing,
- "providing all people of the United States with economic security,
- "promot(ing) justice and equity by stopping current, preventing future, and repairing historic oppression of indigenous peoples, communities of color, migrant communities, deindustrialized communities, depopulated rural communities, the poor, low-income workers, women, the elderly, the unhoused, people with disabilities, and youth (referred to in this resolution as 'frontline and vulnerable communities'),
- "providing resources, training, and high-quality education, including higher education, to all people of the United States, with a focus on frontline and vulnerable communities," all while
- "supporting family farming."

Beyond that, the resolution tackles just about every non-climate-related concern on the environmental agenda, calling for new federal programs to:

- increase soil health,
- provide for a "sustainable food system that ensures universal access to healthy food,

- "restoring and protecting threatened, endangered, and fragile ecosystems through locally appropriate and science-based projects that enhance biodiversity,
- "cleaning up existing hazardous waste and abandoned sites, ensuring economic development and sustainability on those sites," and
- "providing all people of the United States with clean water, clean air, healthy and affordable food, and access to nature."

Republican demagoguery aside, it's unclear what any of that would actually mean in terms of public policy. And that's by design. Maybe "providing all people of the United States with high-quality health care" means a Bernie Sanders Medicare-for-All plan. But it could also mean fixes to the Affordable Care Act. Maybe "providing all people of the United States with economic security" means a $15 federal minimum wage and Universal Basic Income. Or perhaps it simply entails increases in existing welfare programs. The idea, I gather, is to establish where the Green New Deal is going and to politically commit Congress to the trip. The length of the journey (policy ambition) and detailed itinerary (policy design) is TBD based on the political give and take that is to come. This is a resolution after all, not a bill, and that's typically what resolutions are designed to do.

These commitments, however, are so unqualified and open-ended that members don't know what to make of them. That has provided Republicans with an opening to characterize the Green New Deal in the most lurid terms, which has naturally made Democrats deeply uncomfortable. When asked about the Green New Deal on MSNBC's *Morning Joe*, for instance, Sen. Dick Durbin (IL) said, "I've read it and I've reread it and I asked Ed Markey, what in the heck is this?" Speaker Nancy Pelosi has referred to it dismissively as "'The Green Dream,' or whatever they call it. Nobody knows what it is, but they're for it, right?"

There was an FAQ that Rep. Ocasio-Cortez's office emailed to reporters the day her resolution was introduced. That document, however, did not fill in many details. Moreover, it has been mired in controversy and subsequently disavowed by Rep. Ocasio-Cortez and the resolution's co-sponsors, and nothing has been offered in its place. Hence, I can't be sure to what extent even that vague FAQ currently reflects, or ever completely reflected, Green New Dealism.

A useful policy agenda for the Green New Deal was published by Data for Progress, a progressive think tank with ties to Rep. Ocasio-Cortez. But that document is less a translation of the resolution than an exhortation for what some progressives hope might follow from it. Another new progressive think tank with close ties to Rep. Ocasio-Cortez, New Consensus, has published a less granular summary of the thinking behind the Green New Deal, along with a reading list for those who want to dig deeper into the ideas animating it. While both Data for Progress and New Consensus tell us what the progressive community is aiming for with the resolution, they don't necessarily tell us anything about how congressional supporters will interpret these vague Green New Deal goals and objectives.

Rule number one in politics is not to let your opponents define you or your ideas. The vague but suggestive Green New Deal resolution, however, was an open invitation for Republicans to do exactly that. The FAQ and background material coming out of the progressive community gave everyone to your right plenty of ammunition to define you as radicals bent on a sweeping, revolutionary enterprise. "I think the idea is you never let your message get too far out ahead of the substance, and we have definitely created a vacuum and left space for people to fill with what they think the Green New Deal is based on their assumptions and past experiences," conceded Rhiana Gunn-Wright of New Consensus. "It's certainly a danger, but it's a danger worth taking by ensuring we get frontline voices in."

That last line is really the key to understanding the politics animating, and the policies constituting, the Green New Deal. Allow me to try my hand at making the very best case for your strategy as I understand it.

## The Green New Deal Theory of Policy Change

The biggest difficulty associated with tackling climate change is that reducing greenhouse gas emissions imposes very real, very transparent, and very immediate costs with the prospect of benefits that will only become apparent someday down the road. Whatever we might think about the long-term benefits of climate action, in the short-term, it appears to be all cost no matter how much we try to convince voters that there are green jobs, a stronger economy, a healthier planet, or cleaner air and water at the end of the rainbow. Your strategy to overcome that problem is to bury the costs of climate action in a cornucopia of benefits for left-leaning interest groups and to make climate change a central part of the larger progressive program for societal transformation.

This makes some sense. If you can't build a coalition to advance climate action with Republicans, the business community, and the center-right (as noted by political scientist Theda Skocpol, this was the most important lesson learned from the failed Waxman-Markey cap-and-trade initiative in 2009–10), then, per Brad DeLong, you'll have to build it from the left. Given that climate change has never been a very salient issue outside of the environmental community, the policy payoffs to the social justice crowd are the necessary prerequisites for coalition building. Going all-in with this strategy (climate action as the means by which all of the left's political dreams will come true) has the added advantage of harnessing one of the few assets at your disposal to break the reluctance of governing elites (in both parties) to address climate change with the requisite ambition: progressive grassroots power. Given how unlikely it is that the political establishment will ever rise to the challenge and do what's required to stave off climate change (they sure haven't done so yet, and they've been staring at the problem for more than 30 years), a radical disruption of American politics must somehow be brought about. Grassroots action is thus your only option. No matter how long the odds, business-as-usual politics is not going to cut it. We have to throw the long ball. For this to work, you need as many activists as you can get, and they need to be politically weaponized to the greatest extent possible. The scale and scope of the progressive blueprints for the Green New Deal, and the suggestive if vaguely worded Green New Deal resolution, are perfectly designed to do exactly that.

Boiled down, then, your strategy is to create a permanent progressive electoral majority fueled by citizen activism to overwhelm the opposition and stymie any future efforts at repeal. Let's call this "the Grover Norquist total victory theory of policy change," because that's exactly what it is. And I doubt it will work any better for you than it has for him.

While there's a lot wrong with your strategy (which I'll get to in a moment), one of the most important things that I don't think you fully appreciate is that the politics of cost imposition is primarily, as noted by political scientist Kent Weaver, the politics of blame avoidance. Members of Congress don't like imposing pain on their constituents without having some way of breaking what political scientist Douglas Arnold calls the "traceability chain"—the ability of negatively affected constituents to detect costs, trace them to their source, and punish those responsible. The most effective way to do that is bipartisanship. By putting both parties on the record in favor of cost imposition, you make it harder to run against one. Another useful way to break the traceability chain is to play down costs and render them (via clever policy design) opaque and difficult to detect.

Your strategy flirts with disaster by avoiding both approaches. It is nakedly partisan and, to fuel the grassroots movement you're trying to build, implicitly casts costs as a feature, not a bug, of the ambitious and visionary national mobilization you're aiming to achieve. You're betting that the progressive electoral majority that will theoretically come out of this will protect your congressional supporters from any public blowback over costs.

Can this possibly work? No. Let's run through the problems and then turn to what might do the trick.

## Climate Change Is *Not* "Everything Policy"

While there may be a political logic to bundling all of these causes together, there isn't much policy logic to it, and that introduces a host of problems for you.

Your public story for why all of these undertakings need to be tackled as one is because they are all related to one another. I first heard that argument back in 2016 regarding a ballot initiative that would have imposed a carbon tax in the state of Washington. Many progressives actually opposed what would have been the most aggressive climate policy ever adopted in the United States because "viewing climate change as an environmental body of work is way too limited," explained Becky Kelley, president of the Washington Environmental Council and a leader of the progressive opposition. "It's not really an environmental issue, it's a broad, societal and economic issue … Climate policy is not environmental policy. It is everything policy."

Your "it's all related" argument, however, is rather thin. No matter how you feel, for instance, about declining union power in the United States, climate change did not cause a decline in union power, and the climate-related initiatives within the Green New Deal will have little impact on union power one way or the other. Granted, climate change may modestly exacerbate some of the extraneous, non-climate-related problems addressed in the Green New Deal, but if that's true, then reducing greenhouse gas emissions will remedy those harms directly, with no additional policy lifts necessary.

Worse, your "it's all related" argument validates and amplifies misplaced conservative objections to rapid decarbonization. For instance, you argue that a federal jobs guarantee and the like are critical because decarbonization will require immediate and massive transformation of the economy, necessitating federal action to ensure that radically transformed labor markets protect the well-being of millions of displaced workers. Conservative critics of climate action often make that same point in the course of arguing that the cost of decarbonization is staggeringly high.

The labor market dislocations associated with decarbonization, however, are modest at best. According to a macroeconomic modeling exercise discussed in the highly regarded *Risky Business* report, an 80 percent reduction of US greenhouse gas emissions by 2050 (an admittedly less ambitious target than that forwarded by the Green New Deal, but nonetheless a target that puts the United States on a path to doing its share to prevent global warming from exceeding 2 degrees Celsius over preindustrial levels) would likely produce a net increase of hundreds of thousands of jobs right off the bat, with a million or more new jobs created less than two decades hence. These are relatively small numbers in the context of the overall economy, but still, additional federal job-creation measures are unnecessary to accommodate rapid decarbonization.

Similarly, all of your rhetoric about the need for "national mobilization" to put the economy on the equivalent of a wartime footing wildly overstates the level of ambition required to tackle climate change. The same *Risky Business* report calculates that the aforementioned 80 percent reduction of US greenhouse gas emissions by 2050 would require additional capital investments averaging ~$220 billion per year from 2020–2030, $410 billion per year from 2030–2040, and $360 billion per year from 2040–2050. That's an increase of annual, economy-wide investment of between 0.4 and 2 percent of US GDP through 2050. A similar study by Energy and Environmental Economics, Lawrence Berkeley National Laboratory, and the Pacific Northwest National Laboratory found that those reductions would probably cost 0.8 percent of GDP in 2050, with a 50 percent probability the actual number would range from a positive gain of 0.2 percent of GDP to a loss of 1.8 percent of GDP.

To put that in perspective, defense spending associated with World War II amounted to 15.9 percent of US GDP in 1942, 32.2 percent of GDP in 1943, 36 percent of GDP in 1944, and 37.2 percent of GDP in 1945. Rapid decarbonization is a major economic undertaking for sure, but it's nothing remotely close to the economic challenges posed by World War II.

Whether you intend to or not, you are confirming—and raising to a whole new level—unwarranted fear that the cost of addressing climate change is staggeringly high. And no matter how you cut it, high costs do not a useful selling point make.

## Attack of the Killer Watermelons

The Green New Deal resolution quite literally gives a nod to every single last policy demand forwarded by the Democratic Socialists of America. I fear that your "DSA-in-a-box" strategy, however, suggests to the public that conservatives were right all along in charging that climate hawks are political watermelons: green on the outside, red on the inside.

Moreover, you are inadvertently confirming conservative suspicions that you are stoking fears about climate change as a convenient excuse to achieve your real objective: dismantling capitalism as we know it and putting society on a wartime footing under the direction of avowed socialists. While that's an unfair characterization of the motivations of most of the climate activists I know, "solution aversion" and the suspicion that environmentalists are fundamentally hostile to contemporary American society are two key factors fueling conservative opposition to climate action. The design of the Green New Deal, the hastily withdrawn FAQ that accompanied it, and the rhetoric of its most energetic supporters give that argument plausibility. Although conservative objections to the Green New Deal resolution are often overwrought, dishonest, and demagogic, the charge that it is the very definition of radicalism is pretty much on the mark.

While it is certainly true that conservatives would forward the charge of "socialism" and "radicalism" at any meaningful action to address climate change, that doesn't mean it is wise to play into their hands and give them live ammunition for the assault. Unless you are right that the American public longs for "a massive transformation of our society" along the lines suggested by the DSA (which I highly doubt), your strategy entails significant near-term electoral risk. If Democrats lose in 2020 in part because of blowback against the Green New Deal, the larger cause of climate action will be set back for a long time.

Are you really so sure that the gleeful Republican response to the Green New Deal can be waved aside so easily? I understand that easing conservative fears about climate action is not high on your agenda given that your strategy for victory is to simply roll over them. But there are plenty of moderate and center-left voters out there who can easily be moved by these arguments, especially if they are not persuaded climate change is a full-blown crisis. And in fact, your own strategy for rallying progressives suggests that you have still not succeeded in driving home the stakes, even to them. After all, if you have to bribe progressive allies to support climate action by bundling it with measures that have nothing whatsoever to do with climate policy, it suggests that progressives don't really believe their own rhetoric about the urgency of the climate crisis. What else am I to conclude when you tell me that incorporating a federal jobs guarantee, Medicare-for-All, free college, and so forth into the Green New Deal will add support for the initiative?

Republican political strategists certainly seem to think that you've thrown them a political lifeline at a time when they need it most, and there are early signs that charges of Democratic radicalism are gaining traction. A recent public opinion survey from Navigator underscores what common sense would suggest—a political campaign that focuses on climate change without scaring the bejesus out of the public with calls for a national mobilization and a garrison-state economy is an easier sell than what you're marketing at present.

## Magical Thinking Regarding Partisan Power

What, exactly, is your scenario for legislative victory? Passage of the Green New Deal implicitly assumes unified Democratic control of government, but that's not very different from assuming the proverbial can opener. Need I remind you that Democrats have only had unified control of the federal government during two congressional sessions since the election of Ronald Reagan and the full arrival of the conservative movement on the national scene; a grand total of four years out of the last 39? I'll have more to say on that later.

Even if the Democrats accomplish that feat in 2020 (which might be something of a heavy lift), it is impossible to imagine Republicans in the Senate eschewing the filibuster in a fight over the Green New Deal. Where are your 60 votes in the Senate going to come from? I can assure you that they won't be coming from Republicans. Unless we assume a 60+ seat Democratic majority in the Senate (an almost impossible assumption given the Republican lock on rural America), the Green New Deal isn't going anywhere.

But let's posit that the Democrats sweep in 2020 and eliminate the filibuster rule in the Senate. Even under that scenario, your task would prove nearly impossible. Democratic congressional majorities will have been built upon Democratic victories in purple and red districts and states (and not a few fossil fuel states and districts as well), and those Democrats are unlikely to support a legislative package that essentially requires them to abandon appeals to the moderate and conservative voters who got them there. In what world does Sen. Joe Manchin, Sen. John Tester, Sen. Doug Jones, Sen. Sherrod Brown, Sen. Bob Casey, or Sen. Michael Bennet support something like this? Or victorious Democrats in 2020 entering the Senate from, say, Iowa, Georgia, Colorado, Arizona, or North Carolina? At least 10–12 Democratic defections in the Senate doomed the 2009 Waxman-Markey cap-and-trade bill, and that happened when Democrats held 58 seats in the Senate with two Independents who caucused with the party. And that was in response to an infinitely less ambitious climate proposal than the one you're peddling today.

We don't need to speculate about how difficult it will be for you to unite the Democratic caucus. Even this early in the game, despite all of the positive buzz on the left surrounding the Green New Deal, the Democrats in the Senate are loath to vote on the record for the Green New Deal resolution. This ought to tell you something. Moreover, a significant number of important Democrats and coalitional actors have recoiled from the resolution. The 101-member New Democrat Coalition—the largest Democratic caucus in the House—has already signaled their opposition. And perhaps most ominously for your cause, the AFL-CIO has blasted the Green New Deal resolution, calling it "not achievable or realistic."

In sum, the Green New Deal resolution (much less any actual legislation) has a long way to go before it could even win a vote in the Democratic caucus, much less in the United States Congress.

In case you weren't paying attention during the first two years of the Trump administration, it is incredibly difficult to pass legislation (especially ambitious legislation) without a significant degree of bipartisan support, even during those rare periods of unified government. If the legislative record since 1985 is any guide, research by political scientists James Curry and Francis Lee suggests that your chance of passing Green New Deal legislation without Republican support is probably no more than about 4 percent. That's the percentage of the time in which the majority party has advanced high-priority legislation and gotten most of what it wanted over the objections of the majority of the opposing party in both chambers and without the endorsement of at least one elected party leader of the opposing party in either chamber (10 instances out of 254 legislative initiatives).

And if you somehow manage to do so because you eliminated the filibuster rule, you better hold on for dear life. Any Republican congressional majority in the future will be well-positioned to wipe the Green New Deal off the map.

[...]

## Romantic Attachment to Grassroots Activism

I suspect that the reason you're unduly optimistic about your chances of passing the Green New Deal is your belief that ideological tides have decisively turned in your direction and that the old political rules no longer apply. You may be proven correct, but like political scientist Matt Grossmann, I doubt it. I suspect that the present surge in progressive sentiment has less to do with a long-term swing to the progressive left than with the utterly predictable public response—per Stimson—to the most hard-right and politically noxious presidency in modern times.

I've lived this movie before. Back when I was at the Cato Institute and a card-carrying radical of "the Freedom Movement," my fellow libertarians and conservatives were likewise certain that that surge to the right that produced the Gingrich Congress in 1994 was the beginning of the end of the welfare state. Sixteen years later, we thought that the Tea Party's shock troops and the 2010 midterm landslide augured the beginning of "a libertarian moment" that would bring an end to the Great Society and maybe even the New Deal. In 2008, liberals thought their day in the sun had finally arrived with the election of Barack Obama, only to have their hats handed to them in the 2010 midterms, in part because of their passage of the quite-moderate Affordable Care Act.

In these cases, I—like you—read too much into swings in public opinion because it is easy to confuse thermostatic public response to incumbent administrations with secular changes of underlying ideological sentiment. Ideological crusaders easily fall for the notion that they're reliving Paris, 1848. And for some, they're always in Paris and it's always June of 1848. Consequently, they push their political champions to deliver more than is politically possible and overplay their hand.

The reason that mass political uprisings for utopian visions of society are fantasies is that there's a mountain of evidence that the public has no ideology to speak of and no interest whatsoever in having one. We've also known since the groundbreaking work of political scientist Philip Converse that the public has firm, independent, or meaningful opinions about hardly any matters related to public policy. Yet you talk as if climate change will serve as a catalyst for an ideologically charged, DSA-inspired mass electoral uprising.

Organizing interest groups that can mobilize supporters is far more practical than planning for mass electoral uprisings. And happily for you, interest groups can be deployed to good effect even if they represent minority policy preferences (e.g., the political power of the NRA). Unfortunately, you're a long way from having that yet. Being able to mobilize a hundred or so kids for protests in congressional offices is not the same as being able to mobilize millions of voters to pressure politicians to embrace the Green New Deal. As Vox's David Roberts has pointed out, it's extremely difficult in practice to organize a meaningful political grassroots movement around climate action, and doubly difficult to imagine that such a movement can overcome Republican intransigence. And overcoming Republican intransigence is the only way that ambitious climate policy is ever going to come to fruition.

Even so, as political scientist Benjamin Bishin argues, you're not wrong to want to build a vigorous, muscular grassroots movement. You are wrong, however, to think that grassroots activists can force legislators to bend to your will. Grassroots activists can be very effective in stopping legislative initiatives they don't like, but they're far less capable of forcing bills on legislators who are, generally, pretty good at evaluating the political risks of the policies they're asked to vote for.

Policy change is not reliably driven by electoral outcomes or public opinion. It is instead a product of intense insider activity to overcome profound status quo biases in the political system— biases that are not easily moved by external political pressure or material resources. A review of the political histories of the most significant policy changes over the past 70 years (a universe of 790 legislative enactments) finds that only 2.9 percent of the time were public protests and demonstrations credited as a contributing factor in significant policy change. Only 9.4 percent of the time was constituent pressure found to be a factor in the same. And only 11.1 percent of the time was supportive public opinion found to have been a factor in the course of enacting new laws.

Political scientist Matt Grossmann, the author of that study, concludes:

[N]o matter the issue concern, institutionalized entrepreneurs coalescing and compromising within government institutions are the key components of policymaking. I find no issue areas where policy outcomes are primarily a product of public opinion, media coverage, or research trends. Insular policymaking via cooperation among political officials and interest groups is not merely a type of political conflict; it is the typical form of policymaking across the issue spectrum.

"Insular policymaking via cooperation among political officials and interest groups" is what you need. Alas, it's something that you don't seem very interested in.

[...]

## "Half-Baked" Overstates the Cooking

I fear that, by spending so much time upfront taking issue with your strategies and tactics—the problems of which are so profound and interrelated that it takes a lot of time to unpack—I may leave you with the impression that my complaints about the climate policy initiatives forwarded in the Green New Deal are secondary. That is not the case. Despite the fact that I agree completely with your ambition, your sense of urgency, and your desire to fully decarbonize the economy on a rapid pace, you need to rethink how you propose to get from here to there. Because right now, your roadmap for climate action is a hot mess. And I'd warrant that if you gave every well-wishing climate economist and energy policy expert a dose of sodium pentothal, they'd tell you the same thing. Let me count the most obvious problems.

First, regarding your call for net-zero greenhouse gas emissions for the entire energy sector by 2030: If there is any published analysis suggesting that this can be done, please forward it to me, because I can't find any. For an excellent discussion about why this is flatly impossible, see an analysis published this month by J. P. Morgan. Even one of the most knowledgeable and optimistic mavens of the clean energy economy in the world—Michael

Liebreich, founder of Bloomberg New Energy Finance—calls this "an absurd overreach."

Second, you betray your elevation of non-climate-related goals over climate-related goals by appearing to require that renewable fuels constitute 100 percent of all electricity generation 10 years hence, ruling out nuclear power and technologies that capture greenhouse gas emissions from fossil fuel production (called "carbon capture and storage"). Granted, the Green New Deal resolution is ambiguous on this matter, but that ambiguity appears purposeful and thus presents a real problem. These technologies are as climate-friendly as wind and solar power, and they make decarbonization much easier to achieve. If climate change is truly a global emergency (and it is) we need to do everything we can to stop it. Embrace of nuclear power and carbon capture and storage should be made clearly and explicitly.

Third, you leave off the table a host of policy tools that climate hawks routinely reach for when game-planning cost-effective decarbonization. The resolution is silent, for instance, about the critical need for carbon pricing (something that, in case you missed it, is strongly embraced by the very same IPCC reports you routinely cite to justify ambitious climate action). It is likewise silent about the facilitation of denser urban construction, which has a huge impact on greenhouse gas emissions. The resolution has nothing to say about the need to return to the Paris Agreement. It is silent about the need to increase our financial contributions to the developing world to assist in decarbonization abroad.

"How to explain this curious lack of ambition?" asks Jonathan Chait. "Simple: All these things divide progressive activists." Accordingly, "the plan avoids taking stances that are absolutely vital to reduce carbon emissions." This is what naturally follows from a strategy of uni-party coalition building. Every party actor becomes a veto player. One advantage of working across both parties is that fewer groups get to be veto players and thus extract a high price for their cooperation. And the more groups that can extract a high price, the more likely that the whole thing collapses from the weight of all these demands.

I know what you're thinking. "So what if we're not going about decarbonization as 'efficiently' as theoretically possible? We are facing a planetary emergency and don't have the luxury of worrying about cost-effectiveness. Besides, cost-effectiveness has been used as a shield against ambition in the past." But this is precisely why policy design with an eye towards efficiency is critically important. We don't have the resources to waste by misallocating them to costly technologies—or allowing low-cost mitigation opportunities to pass—because doing so meets the political needs of a coalition with other (less important) priorities in mind.

Fourth, the capital costs of your climate-related initiatives would—per Liebriech's counting—be in the ballpark of $1 trillion per year, or a bit shy of 10 percent of national savings; about 5 percent of all economic activity in the United States. As previously noted, that's far, far more than we'd have to spend to accomplish those same goals on a mid-century timetable. And that's before we take into consideration the cost of universal housing guarantees, universal job guarantees, universal education guarantees, universal income guarantees, federal paid family and vacation leave, and so forth. There's no way of intelligently guessing what that might all cost, so I'm not going to bother.

Fifth, your means of paying for all of this is to simply print currency and to heck with inflation and the national debt. This financial recklessness comes out of your interpretation of "modern monetary theory," a school of thought that I suspect you may not understand as well as you think you do. It has been fiercely criticized by just about every mainstream economist who has offered an opinion (e.g., Paul Krugman, Larry Summers, Ken Rogoff, and Scott Sumner), and even by the leftists at *Jacobin* magazine. Ironically, your reply to this criticism is that neoliberal economists have been wrong before about a lot of things, so we shouldn't defer to them to now. Has it occurred to you, however, that this is the exact same argument that climate deniers use in the scientific arena (scientists have been wrong before about a lot of things in the past, so they shouldn't be deferred to now)? I suggest that if you want to take seriously the consensus of experts (and you should), you don't do so only when it's politically convenient. Otherwise, you show yourselves to be no different than your opponents.

Sixth, it might surprise you to learn that I agree that, per economist Dani Rodrik, there's a strong theoretical case for using industrial policy to facilitate the development of zero-carbon technologies (a defining characteristic of the Green New Deal), especially when undertaken explicitly. My hair stands up, however, when I learn that you propose to do this via "democratic and participatory processes that are inclusive of and led by frontline and vulnerable communities and workers to plan, implement, and administer the Green New Deal mobilization at the local level." How would that work exactly? We don't have any examples of industrial policy done through democratic and participatory mechanisms. They're typically done by technocratic elites serving in agencies with a high degree of bureaucratic insulation. In the United States, for instance, the best example is DARPA. Forgive me if I'm skeptical about complex, technical planning exercises by front-line activists undertaken in this fashion.

I've seen all of this before. When zealots of whatever stripe enter the realm of public policy, they almost invariably gravitate towards the weakest arguments, the dodgiest data, the most problematic theories, and the most dubious but convenient set of assumptions. That's because the ends are so morally compelling (to them) that their interest in engaging in due diligence regarding arguments they desperately want to believe naturally flies out the window. If you don't have a skeptical mind when you encounter arguments that you want to believe, you're going find yourself believing a whole lot of politically convenient nonsense.

# You're Wasting Valuable Time

It is absolutely critical that we have a well-vetted, politically attractive, ready-for-prime-time legislative package ready for the 117th Congress if a window of opportunity opens after the 2020 election. Putting together ambitious legislation like this, however, takes years. A center of political gravity needs to be created around one of the many possible ways forward so that climate activists are united. Influential stakeholders outside of the NGO community need to be fully bought-in. Complex policy matters need to be carefully thought through, requiring an iterative process of engagement with hundreds of various political and policy experts given the dispersal of knowledge. Politically critical trade-offs need to be experimented with and tested. Preliminary iterations of the package need to be debated in public in order to modify proposals in response to feedback. Politicians need to be made comfortable with the package, and for the typical, risk-averse politician, comfort takes time to build when so much political capital is on the line.

The intense political and policy negotiations, compromises, and analyses required to do all of this occur primarily in the context of drafting actual legislation. That is why successful legislative initiatives are usually iterative products of legislation introduced in previous Congresses. If we're going to pass ambitious climate legislation in the 117th Congress, a preliminary iteration of whatever we're going to put forward had best be introduced in a serious fashion (not via a messaging bill, where most of these issues are ducked) in the 116th Congress.

Unfortunately, I see few signs of that happening. Instead, I see a replay of the failed efforts to pass health care reform in previous Congresses. In 1977–1978, for instance, a clear window of political opportunity was open for health care reform, but liberal health care advocates were split on what reform ought to look like. Before they could resolve matters, the window of political opportunity unexpectedly closed with the 1978 midterm elections, and, to their chagrin, it did not open again for more than a decade. In 1993, the window of opportunity for health care reform finally opened again, but health care advocates had failed to do the necessary work in the intervening 15 years. The Clinton administration tried to put together a health care reform package on the fly, but was unable to successfully do so before the window of opportunity closed once again with the 1994 midterm elections. It took another 14 years for the window of opportunity to open again with the election of Barack Obama, but this time, the experience of passing and then implementing "Romney-Care" in Massachusetts provided the well-vetted political and policy template for federal action that had eluded health care advocates in the past. The result was the Affordable Care Act (ACA) in 2010. Conservative health care advocates, for their part, schemed immediately to undo the ACA, but they did little to come up with a well-vetted, politically viable alternative to the ACA during their eight years in the wilderness over the course of the Obama administration. When the window of opportunity unexpectedly opened for them in 2017, they had nothing viable to put on the political table, and the Republican attempt to put something together on the fly predictably failed before their window of opportunity closed with the midterm elections of 2018.

As the health care reform experience well demonstrates, the political stars rarely align for major policy change, and when they do, they do not align for long. Do yourself a favor and pick up a copy of political scientist John Kingdon's *Agendas, Alternatives, and Public Policies* (2nd Edition), where the story I'm telling you is forwarded with full analytic and empirical force. Read it twice. Time spent chasing the Green New Deal magic pony is time taken away from the serious vetting that is necessary to put a plausible legislative program together. And it also increases the pressure on such a program by raising expectations among advocates of what can actually be done, meaning a serious program could very well die under accusations of ideological betrayal.

I know what you're thinking. "You do you. I'll do me. And we'll see what works." But you're demanding a one-way street.

Politicians who are interested in other paths are being protested by New Green Deal activists, slandered in the media, and threatened with primary challenges. Democratic congressional leaders have been pressured (thankfully, unsuccessfully) to force legislative work strictly down a Green New Deal path. Presidential candidates are required to bend the knee to the Green New Deal in return for progressive support. You're trying in every way you can to eliminate political oxygen for prospective allies who are interested in exploring different paths.

Moreover, by rallying progressives to maximalist demands completely unmoored from political reality, you are making it difficult to imagine a broad-based alliance for climate action coming to fruition before the 2020 election. If progressives fail to work productively with moderates in the course of drafting prospective legislation (in this Congress!), I can guarantee you that any opportunity for climate action will be missed in the 117th Congress, and who knows when the next window of political opportunity might present itself.

You say, "Well, we can always negotiate back if we hit a political wall." But it sure doesn't seem to me that your activists are a "walk it back" kind of crowd. When you unleash magical political thinking and mix it with ideological fervor and policy maximalism, you don't create a promising environment for compromise. The Tea Party and Freedom Caucus experience should warn you off the conceit that party establishments can turn militant extremism on and off at will.

In any case, it takes time to negotiate compromises; sometimes, years. It can't be done on the fly in the teeth of a legislative defeat. It would seem to me that, with the AFL-CIO and the New Democrat Coalition now arrayed against you, it might be a good time to recognize a political wall for what it is and hit the reset button (at least, behind the scenes) so that something might productively come out of the next Congress.

These are high stakes you're playing. You're absolutely right that we are about out of time if we want to meaningfully address the oncoming climate emergency. We don't have another decade to lose waiting for future windows of opportunity to open.

[…]

Your role in moving climate legislation is absolutely critical: to forcefully remind Democrats that modest, incremental half-measures are insufficient. I'm a great proponent of moderation, but in the climate arena, Andrew Sullivan is correct: moderation dictates radical action. While political reality may well prevent us from doing all that we should (politics usually works that way), we can take solace in the fact that even half-measures will reduce climate risks and damages by equal measure. And given what's likely in store for the planet, that's not nothing.

I've spent a great deal of time here criticizing the path you're on, but the most important thing you've done right is to elevate climate change to the top of the progressive agenda while making a strong moral case for action. The left has never cared enough about climate change to make it a political priority, and you're the main reason for the Democratic Party's renewed interest in ambitious climate action. You've also helped force the beginning of a Republican rethink about the political merits of climate denial, incentivized Republican legislators to offer their own ideas about climate policy, and encouraged more policy ambition on their part than might otherwise have been the case (although their devastating loss of the House due to defections by college-educated moderates in the suburbs, along with the work of organizations like mine to move Republicans into a better place on climate, likely had an impact as well).

Calls for radical action are not self-executing. Effective radicalism requires political realism. You need allies to enact your agenda. I want what you want (at least, on the climate front). But I want to win, and while I don't have all the answers about how best to do that, history gives us a pretty good sense of what not to do if our cause is going to prevail when a window of political opportunity next opens.

# Periodical and Internet Sources Bibliography

*The following articles have been selected to supplement the diverse views presented in this chapter.*

Natalie Bennett, "Mapping Out the Green Party's Future," *The Guardian*, May 2016. https://www.theguardian.com /politics/2016/may/18/mapping-out-the-green-party-future

Democratic Audit UK, "When Are Green Parties Successful?" Democratic Audit, November 30, 2018. https://www .democraticaudit.com/2018/11/30/when-are-green-parties -successful/

Amien Essif, "US Green Party: 'There's More at Stake Than Getting Rid of Trump,'" DW, October 26, 2020. https://www.dw.com /en/us-green-party-theres-more-at-stake-than-getting-rid-of -trump/a-55399856

Adam Gabbatt, "'A Big Victory Would Be 5%': Green Party's Howie Hawkins Eyes Progress," *The Guardian*, August 14, 2020. https:// www.theguardian.com/us-news/2020/aug/14/howie-hawkins -green-party-interview-us-elections

Ted Glick, "Does the US Green Party Have a Future?" https://tedglick .com/future-hope-columns/does-the-us-green-party-have-a -future/

Green Party of the United States, "Elections." https://gpus.org /elections/

Howie Hawkins, "Replace the Electoral College with a Ranked-Choice National Popular Vote for President," Green Party US, December 14, 2020. https://www.gp.org/replace_electoral_college

A. J. Krow, "I'm Proud of Voting Green Party in 2020," Medium, October 15, 2020. https://medium.com/genius-in-a-bottle/im -proud-of-voting-green-party-in-2020-e764f1688ab2

Bill McKibben, "Instead of Challenging Joe Biden, Maybe the Green Party Could Help Change Our Democracy," *New Yorker*, April 14, 2020. https://www.newyorker.com/news/daily-comment/instead -of-challenging-joe-biden-maybe-the-green-party-could-help -change-our-democracy

Luigi Morris, "No Good Choices: How the Two-Party System Fails Voters," *Left Voice*, November 13, 2020. https://www.leftvoice.org /no-good-choices-how-the-two-party-system-fails-voters/

Alex Phillips, "The Green Party's Future Is to the Left of Labour," Bright Green, July 8, 2020. http://bright-green.org/2020/07/08 /the-green-partys-future-is-to-the-left-of-labour/

Tobias Gerhard Schminke, "The Present and Future of the Green Wave—Part 2: The Future," Heinrich Böll Stiftung, January 18, 2021. https://eu.boell.org/index.php/en/2021/01/18/present-and -future-green-wave-part-2-future

Dan Solomon, "Does the Green Party Matter?" *Texas Monthly*, August 8, 2016. https://www.texasmonthly.com/the-daily-post /green-party-matter/

Nick Troiano, "Why America Doesn't Have the Third Party It Wants," *The Hill*, February 20, 2021. https://thehill.com/opinion /campaign/539731-why-america-doesnt-have-the-third-party-it -wants

# For Further Discussion

## Chapter 1

1. Should governments implement policies to better protect the environment?
2. Should the Green Party focus on its environmental platform or on a broader platform? Why?
3. How important are environmental issues when it comes to choosing a party or a candidate to support?

## Chapter 2

1. Why might people support politicians to the right, to the left, or at the center?
2. Should political parties try to work within the current system or try to drastically change that system?
3. How can politicians balance environmental protections with people's needs and desires for a comfortable lifestyle?

## Chapter 3

1. How important is it for America to have additional parties besides the Republican and Democratic Parties?
2. Should third parties be added to the major debates for presidential candidates? If so, under what criteria?
3. Should campaign financing rules be changed? If so, why and how?

## Chapter 4

1. Should America's Electoral College process change? If so, how?
2. Should third parties get public funding to support their election campaigns? If so, under what conditions?
3. Should the Green Party focus more on running a presidential candidate or on local elections? Explain.

# Organizations to Contact

*The editors have compiled the following list of organizations concerned with the issues debated in this book. The descriptions are derived from materials provided by the organizations. All have publications or information available for interested readers. The list was compiled on the date of publication of the present volume; the information provided here may change. Be aware that many organizations take several weeks or longer to respond to inquiries, so allow as much time as possible.*

## The Democratic Party

430 South Capitol Street SE
Washington, DC 20003
contact form: democrats.org/contact-us
website: www.democrats.org

The Democratic National Committee attempts to elect Democrats at every level of politics. On the website, learn about its party platform and stands on the issues.

## Green Left

PO Box 394, Broadway
NSW 2007
Australia
contact form: www.greenleft.org.au/contact
website: www.greenleft.org.au

This Australian site says, "We seek to help the organising efforts of all those actively resisting the increasingly authoritarian rule of the corporate rich, here and overseas." Check out news and analysis from around the world.

## Green Party of the United States

PO Box 75075
Washington, DC 20013
(202) 319-7191
email: office@gp.org
contact form: https://www.gp.org/contact
website: www.gp.org

View recent news articles, learn why people have chosen to join the Green Party, and learn about activism. The site says, "We are grassroots activists, environmentalists, advocates for social justice, nonviolent resisters and regular citizens who've had enough of corporate-dominated politics."

## Library of Congress

101 Independence Avenue SE
Washington, DC 20540
(202) 707-5000
contact form: ask.loc.gov
website: www.loc.gov/classroom-materials/elections
/presidential-election-process

The Library of Congress is the main research arm of the US Congress. Learn about the presidential election process. The Political Parties page explores "the many political parties that have played a role in American presidential elections."

## openDemocracy

The Print House
18 Ashwin Street
London, E8 3DL
United Kingdom
+44 (0)20 7459 4068
email: info@opendemocracy.net
website: opendemocracy.net/en

OpenDemocracy is an independent global media organization. Learn about its projects and read news from around the world on topics such as the environment, economics, racism, gender and sexuality, and more.

### People's World

3339 S. Halsted Street
Chicago, IL 60608
(773) 446-9920
contact form: www.peoplesworld.org/contact
website: www.peoplesworld.org
People's World is a voice for progressive change and socialism in the United States. It provides news and analysis of the labor and democratic movements.

### Pew Research Center

1615 L Street NW, Suite 800
Washington, DC 20036
(202) 419-4300
website: www.pewresearch.org

Pew Research Center conducts public opinion polling and other data-driven social science research. Research topics include politics and policy.

### Republican National Committee

310 First Street SE
Washington, DC 20003
(202) 863-8500
website: www.gop.com

The Republican National Committee supports Republican politicians. Learn about its platform and viewpoint on various issues, such as the economy, energy and the environment, and elections.

## Sightline Institute

1402 Third Avenue, Suite 500
Seattle, WA 98101
(206) 447-1880
contact form: https://www.sightline.org/about/contact-us
website: www.sightline.org

Sightline Institute is an independent, nonprofit research and communications center for the Pacific Northwest US. On the website, learn about its research, including topics such as climate and energy.

## Truthdig

1158 26th Street, No. 443
Santa Monica, CA 90403-4698
contact form: ruthdig.com/contact
website: www.truthdig.com

Truthdig "is dedicated to reporting on current issues that are insufficiently covered by mainstream media." The site has an archive "of 15 years of award-winning independent journalism" available for free. Check out news and opinions on the environment and many other political and social issues.

## Unite America

1580 Lincoln Street, Suite 520
Denver, CO 80203
(720) 592-0843
email: hello@uniteamerica.org
website: www.uniteamerica.org

Unite America is a grassroots organization "with the goal of reforming the political system and bridge the partisan divide. Unite America supports both electoral political reforms as well as independent-minded candidates."

## US Political Parties & Organizations

website: www.aascu.org/programs/adp/votingresources /politicalparties.pdf

The American Association of State Colleges and Universities provides "a list of established political parties and organizations in the United States along with their platforms and/or values."

## World Socialist Web Site (WSWS)

contact: https://www.wsws.org/en/special/pages/contact.html website: www.wsws.org/en

The WSWS calls itself "the authoritative voice of international revolutionary socialism." The website provides articles, videos, and podcasts on history, class struggle, capitalism, inequality, and other political subjects.

# Bibliography of Books

Kate Aronoff. *Overheated: How Capitalism Broke the Planet—And How We Fight Back.* New York, NY: Bold Type Books, 2021.

Kate Aronoff. *A Planet to Win: Why We Need a Green New Deal.* Brooklyn, NY: Verso, 2019.

Michael Barone. *How America's Political Parties Change (and How They Don't).* New York, NY: Encounter Books, 2019.

Noam Chomsky and Robert Pollin. *Climate Crisis and the Global Green New Deal: The Political Economy of Saving the Planet.* Brooklyn, NY: Verso, 2020.

Jessamyn Conrad. *What You Should Know About Politics . . . But Don't, Fourth Edition: A Nonpartisan Guide to the Issues That Matter.* New York, NY: Arcade, 2020.

Stan Cox. *The Green New Deal and Beyond: Ending the Climate Emergency While We Still Can.* San Francisco, CA: City Lights Publishers, 2020.

Elizabeth R. DeSombre. *What Is Environmental Politics?* Hoboken, NJ: Wiley, 2020.

Lee Drutman. *Breaking the Two-Party Doom Loop: The Case for Multiparty Democracy in America.* Oxford, UK: Oxford University Press, 2019.

Howie Hawkins. *Independent Politics: The Green Party Strategy Debate.* Chicago, IL: Haymarket Books, 2006.

Robert C. Hockett. *Financing the Green New Deal: A Plan of Action and Renewal.* London, UK: Palgrave Macmillan, 2020.

Larry Jordan. *The Green New Deal: Why We Need It And Can't Live Without It—And No, It's Not Socialism!* Chula Vista, CA: Page Turner Books International, 2019.

Naomi Klein. *On Fire: The (Burning) Case for a Green New Deal*. New York, NY: Simon & Schuster, 2019.

David L. Lewis. *Science for Sale: How the US Government Uses Powerful Corporations and Leading Universities to Support Government Policies, Silence Top Scientists, Jeopardize Our Health, and Protect Corporate Profits*. New York, NY: Skyhorse Publishing, 2019.

Marc Morano. *Green Fraud: Why the Green New Deal Is Even Worse Than You Think*. Washington, DC: Regnery Publishing, 2021.

Ann Pettifor. *The Case for the Green New Deal*. Brooklyn, NY: Verso, 2019.

Varshini Prakash and Guido Girgenti. *Winning the Green New Deal: Why We Must, How We Can*. New York, NY: Simon & Schuster, 2020.

Jeremy Rifkin. *The Green New Deal: Why the Fossil Fuel Civilization Will Collapse by 2028, and the Bold Economic Plan to Save Life on Earth*. New York, NY: St. Martin's Press, 2019.

Steven J. Rosenstone, Roy L. Behr, and Edward H. Lazarus. *Third Parties in America: Citizen Response to Major Party Failure*. Princeton, NJ: Princeton University Press, 2018.

Alan F. Zundel. *The Creation of the Green Party of the United States...And Its Neglect of a Strategic Dilemma*. Independently published, 2020.

# Index